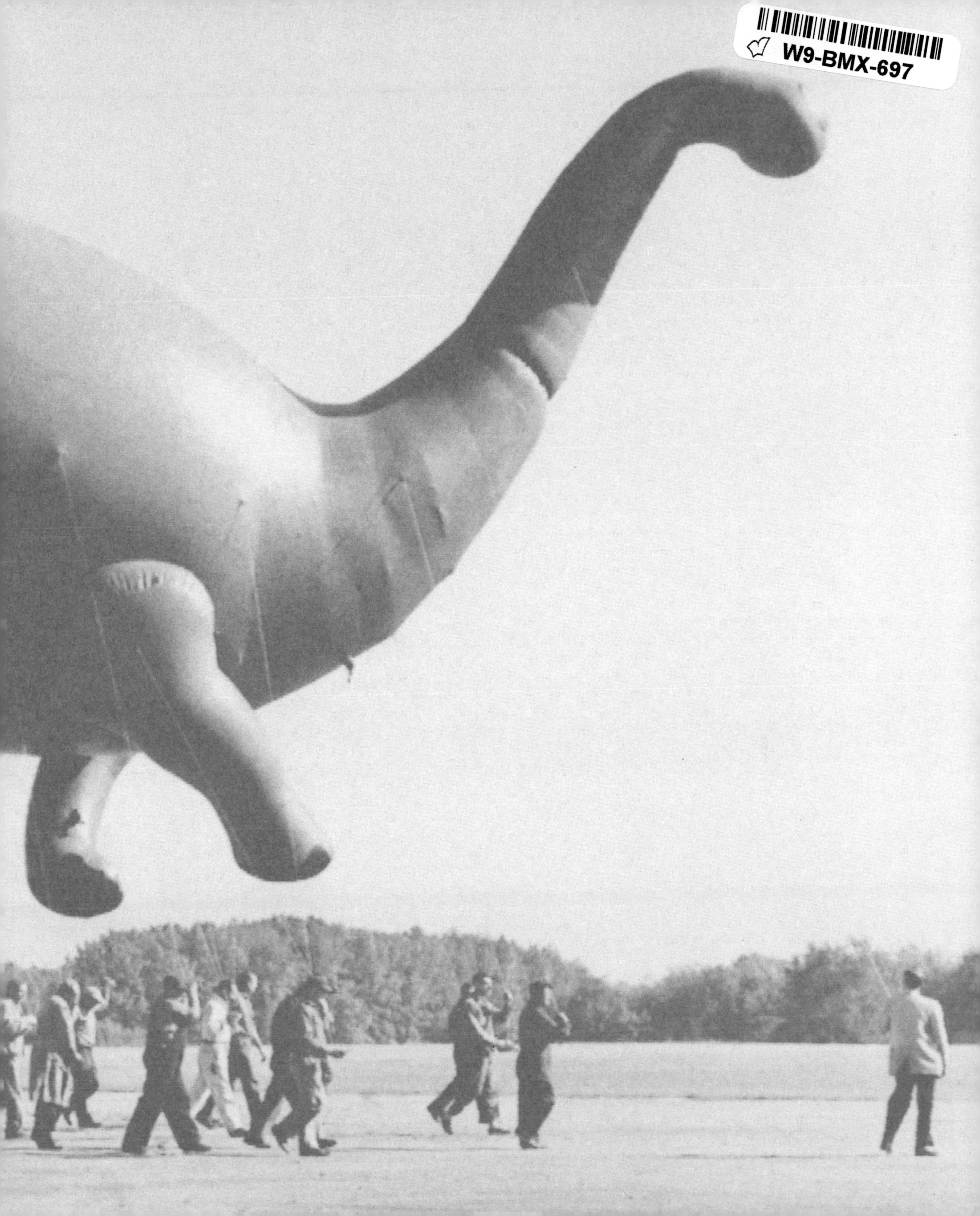

America's Parade

A Celebration of Macy's Thanksgiving Day Parade

America's Parade

A Celebration of Macy's Thanksgiving Day Parade

LIFE

Editor Robert Sullivan
Art Director Ian Denning
Picture Editor Barbara Baker Burrows
Senior Editor Robert Andreas
Associate Picture Editor Donna F. Aceto
Senior Reporter Hildegard Anderson
Writer Stephen Madden
Copy Chief Pamela Warren
Production Manager Michael H. Roseman
Picture Researchers Gillian Harper, Joan Shweky

General Manager Andrew Blau
Finance Director Camille Sanabria

**Time Inc.
Home Entertainment**

President
Rob Gursha

**Vice President,
Branded Businesses**
David Arfine

**Executive Director,
Marketing Services**
Carol Pittard

**Director, Retail
& Special Sales**
Tom Mifsud

Director of Finance
Tricia Griffin

Marketing Director
Kenneth Maehlum

Assistant Director
Ann Marie Ross

**Editorial Operations
Manager**
John Calvano

**Associate Product
Managers**
Jennifer Dowell,
Meredith Shelley

**Assistant Product
Manager**
Michelle Kuhr

Special thanks to:
Victoria Alfonso,
Suzanne DeBenedetto,
Robert Dente, Gina
Di Meglio, Peter Harper,
Roberta Harris, Natalie
McCrea, Jessica McGrath,
Jonathan Polsky, Emily
Rabin, Mary Jane Rigoroso,
Steven Sandonato,
Tara Sheehan, Bozena
Szwagulinski, Marina
Weinstein, Niki Whelan

LIFE would like to thank
Bob Rutan, who manages
Macy's archive, and Robin
Hall, the current Director
of Macy's Parade, for
their research assistance
throughout the
production of this book.

Copyright 2001
Time Inc. Home
Entertainment

Published by

LIFE Books

Time Inc.
1271 Avenue of the
Americas
New York, New York 10020

ISBN: 1-929049-43-9
Library of Congress
Catalogue Number:
2001091491

"LIFE" is a trademark of
Time Inc.

We welcome your
comments and suggestions
about LIFE Books.
Please write to us at:
LIFE Books
Attention: Book Editors
PO Box 11016
Des Moines, IA 50336-1016

If you would like to order
any of our hardcover
Collector's Edition books,
please call us at 1-800-327-
6388 (Monday through
Friday, 7:00 a.m.–8:00 p.m.
or Saturday, 7:00 a.m.–
6:00 p.m. Central Time).

Please visit our website at
www.TimeBookstore.com

Front endpaper photo:
AP/Wide World
Back endpaper photo:
New York Daily News

This page: Escorting the Tree along
Convent Avenue in the mid-1920s.
Previous three pages: Majorette
and band herald the Turkey, 1959;
Betty Boop takes in—and over—
Central Park, 1988.
Front endpaper: An Apatosaurus
trains in Ohio for the big day, 1969.
Back endpaper: Santa glides past
an enticing chimney on Central
Park West, 1940.

More Than Just a Parade

Foreword by Willard Scott

For 11 years, I was the host of the Macy's Thanksgiving Day Parade on NBC television. It was the only job I ever dreamed of doing. For sure, when I was a kid I had ambitions other than the parade, but deep down in my heart this was the one great secret wish. And I had made it come true.

Macy's Thanksgiving Day Parade is so much more than just a parade. Along with the tree in Rockefeller Center and all the storefronts with their decorations, the parade really is a kickoff for the holiday season. If you please, it is New York City's great gift to America and now, with satellite television, the entire world. Literally millions of people turn on the TV at nine o'clock a.m. Eastern time on Thanksgiving Day not merely to watch, but to experience the tradition of this event. We all share this modern day communion of sorts, creating memories that last as long as we live. Thanksgiving may just be the one spiritual holiday that we share. Our families, all together, the smell and activities that come from the kitchen, the anticipation of the turkey on the table, the pies, right down to passing the Russell Stover box after the feast and, of course, the spirit of thankfulness for all that we have, a spirit that comes down to us from the Pilgrims.

Yes, indeed, there is a special magic on that particular day, all the way from West 77th Street on Central Park down Broadway to 34th. For three enchanting hours, the Macy's Thanksgiving Day Parade weaves its spell. The police on the street, the Macy's employees, the NBC crew, the thousands of cheerleaders, band members, Broadway musical casts, the celebrities who wave from the floats, and the balloons—all given out with a little something extra special on this extra special day. There is a spirit in the air that comes from within all of us who have ever had the privilege of being part of this parade.

When as a young boy I chose this dream to be a goal in my life, I chose well. Every year, old memories are recalled, while new memories are made as new generations come to make the parade a part of their life. You can sense the excitement of these newcomers as the hour nears: "Let the Parade Begin!" And let me add: "May It Never End."

Willard Scott

In 1959, a year after the Rockettes' debut in the parade, these roller skaters had a rockier time as they were pursued by Rocket Man.

From the first floats to the coming of "falloons," from the year a flyaway pig got snared over Brooklyn through the years of wind and weather, here's the spirited saga of a beloved American institution.

The Magical History of Macy's Miracle on 34th Street

Let's

Have a Parade!

t began as a way to celebrate America. This parade, so large today and so beloved—more than a dozen bands, more than a dozen giant balloons and 8,000 marchers strong; viewed annually by 2.5 million people in New York and 65 million nationwide—had a poignant genesis in 1924 when a group of Macy's employees, many of them first-generation immigrants, sought a way to express gratitude for their new, vibrant American heritage. They reflected upon the festive holiday celebrations of their native lands, and then considered the upcoming, quintessentially American holiday known as Thanksgiving. Might we, they asked the boss, have a festival on Thanksgiving, one that could herald the coming of Christmas?

Might we have a parade?

The boss was not Rowland Hussey Macy. Despite the implications of the famous 1947 movie about the parade, *Miracle on 34th Street*, there was at the time no "Mr. Macy." There had been one, of course, but Mr. Macy was long gone by 1924, never mind 1947. Born on the Massachusetts island of Nantucket in 1822, the Quaker R.H. Macy put to sea as a cabin boy on a whaler, came home, settled on the mainland, tried his hand as a merchant in Boston and California, then in 1858 opened his fancy dry-goods store in New York City. When his prosperous enterprise evolved into a genuine

★ **Macy's wasn't at all shy about trumpeting its yet-untried parade, knowing that it had two aces in the hole: the marionette-maker Tony Sarg and the ringmaster Charles Donner.**

department store, Macy brought aboard Isidor Straus to run the glassware and china concession. Mr. Macy died in Paris in 1877, and the stewardship of the store eventually passed to descendants of Straus. By the time eager employees were asking for their parade, the president was Herbert Straus, and it was he who announced, at a November luncheon in 1924, that Macy's was shortly to present an incredible show that would set the city on its ear.

He was right from the start. Whether or not the first parade director shouted "Let's have a parade!" to kick things off (as all directors do today, following hallowed tradition), we do not know. What we do know of that inaugural event includes bits of statistical history, some arcana and lots of lore.

We'll start with the facts.

Macy's first Thanksgiving Day Parade was held on November 27, 1924. It began way up in Harlem at 145th Street, more than three miles farther north than the modern start line. The marchers included about a thousand Macy's employees, plus spectators who joined in. The nearly six-mile route ran down Convent and Morningside avenues from 145th Street to 110th Street, west to Broadway, south to Columbus Circle, south on Eighth Avenue to 40th Street, west on 40th to Broadway and south to Macy's Herald Square store. (Today's mammoth parade, 2.5 miles long, largely avoids all the sharp twists and turns.) While the earliest advertisements talked of a one p.m. start time, this was changed to nine a.m. in the days leading up to Thanksgiving, and word certainly got out. "Something like a million" New Yorkers attended, according to the *Newark Ledger*. More reliable estimates have 250,000 spectators lining the route.

The thousands were wondering as one if the parade could possibly live up to Mr. Straus's promise, and to those of a series of gushing newspaper ads: "A Magnificent Holiday Event ... A SURPRISE NEW YORK WILL NEVER FORGET!"

In putting itself on the line like this, Macy's knew it had a secret weapon. Charles Donner, the store's assistant superintendent of delivery, had worked for a circus. Now the parade offered him an ideal opportunity to revive dormant skills.

The parade was a mere two blocks in length,

but it packed a big top's worth of entertainment. A troupe of 35 clowns did handstands and tumbled down the avenues. There were zoo animals of several stripes—elephants, camels, goats, donkeys—although, because the parade would pass under an elevated subway line, giraffes were left behind. There were knights in armor, sheiks, a princess. There was a jazz band made up of Macy's African-American employees. There was something called a "conceit squad": people wearing grotesquely huge heads. In a nod to old R.H. himself, there were folks dressed as Quakers (not the last time Quaker and/or Nantucket motifs would be included in the parade). There were floats featuring Mother Goose characters. And, beginning a tradition nev-

★ **Miss Muffet, played by a Macy's employee and plagued by a spider (but otherwise enjoying the lovely day), rode her tuffet in the very first Thanksgiving parade.**

er to be interrupted, there was a marching band. Glitches were few. A white steed that was supposed to lead the Ben-Hur float went missing at the 11th hour, and the festive procession caused traffic jams at nearly every intersection. Neither circumstance detracted from the overall euphoria, and the day was judged a splendid success. Wrote the *Ledger:* "Macy's officials must have felt like life was worth living after all, to see those swarms of hooting, enthusiastic children and the entire crowd carried into ecstasies of delight." When Santa's float arrived at the store and the great elf was crowned King of the Kiddies, then ensconced on a golden throne above the Macy's marquee, a mighty cheer went up from the 10,000 jammed onto 34th Street. Even with

Santa's ascension, the day was not done. Shades were drawn on a 75-foot-long window, and the fabulous Wondertown display was revealed. The crowd pressed forward to view hundreds of animated marionettes in 26 separate scenes. Over there, Little Jack Horner was sticking his thumb into a pie; down there, Little Bo Peep was tending her sheep; and there, Old Mother Hubbard was giving her dog a bone. The fantastic set piece was the product of a yearlong effort by puppeteer, designer and soon-to-be-balloonmaker Tony Sarg, who can be seen these years later as the creative father of the Macy's Thanksgiving Day Parade.

Final points to clear up: There were no balloons in that first parade. And while Macy's now rightly prides itself on staging the parade come rain or shine, in 1924 it stood ready with a rain

★ Sarg was Macy's Mr. Everything. He designed much of the parade. He designed a fantasyland that drew throngs to the store's 34th Street windows (right). Then he designed and drew newspaper ads to promote the show, not forgetting the crucial postscript: "Macy's for Gifts."

★ **In 1926, horse-drawn floats were still the principal attractions, while many small balloons were mere portents of bigger—much bigger—things to come in 1927.**

date of Friday, and said so in the papers (therefore, its remarkable record of "every Thanksgiving but the war years" was in jeopardy even before it began). Finally, Macy's was not, contrary to legend, the first department-store parade, nor the first Christmas parade. In fact, Macy's rival, the Gimbel brothers, had organized a parade of toys in Philadelphia in 1920.

★ ★ ★ ★ ★

The ideas and traditions of parading are manifold, and it is interesting to see where Macy's pageant, now so much a part of our national fabric, fits in.

People marching down a town's main thoroughfares to honor a joyful or solemn occasion is an ancient happening: The origins of the modern parade date to around 3000 B.C. On the walls of the pyramids there are pictures of formal processions and of armies marching. Rome elevated the parade to an art form at approximately the time of Christ. Elaborate streets with grand arches were constructed as settings for "triumphs" that would honor military victories. The most popular forms of parade even then, however, were those that featured circus performers.

Festival parades evolved to something resembling their present shape about 500 years ago in Europe. As the Middle Ages ended and the Renaissance dawned, religious commemoration of a saint's feast day might well involve a parade. So, too, there were celebrations of pagan traditions, of the seasons, of great events such as the arrival of a monarch or envoy. The revelry we now associate with parades became a welcome staple.

Parades came to America before there was a United States. Swedish immigrants who settled outside Philadelphia were shooting off muskets in their annual Mummers Parade in the early 1700s. In 1762, Irish soldiers marched to the Battery in New York City on Saint Patrick's Day, starting a tradition. (An irony is that the men were serving in the militia of Ireland's arch-enemy, Britain.) There were parades to mark the birth of nationhood, and parades to mark the end of the Civil War. Two parades that rival Macy's as events commanding the nation's attention were born in the 1800s: In 1837 Mardi Gras began as a street parade in New Orleans, and in 1890 the Valley Hunt Club of Pasadena, California, staged a Battle of Flowers that would blossom, not long thereafter, as the Tournament of Roses Parade.

It was Macy's accidental genius that it borrowed the most attractive enticements from many parades, without emphasizing any to such a degree that it became a parochial or exclusive affair. It wanted to look good but wasn't just about flowers. It wanted to be a party but not a saturnalia. In that it drew from many native cultures, it was gently political but it was hardly just for, say, the Irish or the Italians. It was about Christmas, yes, but in the oblique, even ecumenical, way that Mardi Gras was about Lent. Christmas gave Macy's a reason, but wasn't the only reason. Thanksgiving Day—an American invention, as we will shortly see—was as central to the parade's ethos as was Christmas. So the parade was energetic, spirited, showy, democratic, secular and nonsecular. It looked like America.

And it clicked, right off the bat. "The longest day those kids will live, they will see in their golden dreams of youthful days that happiness of yesterday," gushed the *Ledger* on the day after Thanksgiving in 1924. With others offering comparable journalistic hosannas, the door was open for Macy's itself to engage in some auto–back-patting. In an ad that ran in the *Herald Tribune,* the store thanked all New Yorkers "for the overwhelming interest and festive enthusiasm which helped us make yesterday's Christmas Parade such a magnificent spectacle … The tremendous ovation which you accorded to yesterday's procession has led us to decide that, barring unforeseen obstacles … " Cue the boldface type, Mr. Conductor: **"Such a parade will hereafter be an** annual feature of Macy's Christmas program for the people. We advise you now to make no other engagements for the morning of Thanksgiving Day, 1925."

Few disobeyed, and Macy's disappointed no one as it expanded and improved the parade in the next few years. If the spontaneity—the "Hey, kids, let's put on a show!" feel—of the employees' parade went missing, this was more than compensated for by a professionalized effort at extravaganza. Room in Macy's Long Island warehouse was set aside for the construction of floats, which grew in size and number. A tent was erected on 110th Street so that the parade could be assembled overnight.

In 1925, Santa was accompanied by 25 Snow Babies, female employees dressed in fur-trimmed parkas. At Herald Square he delivered the crowd to the latest Sarg window spectacular, "A Thousand and One Nights," which told the *Arabian Nights* story in 26 scenes. There

were five bands that year, and one float featured, according to the *Times,* "a laughing caterpillar, 100 feet long, which writhed and wriggled down the line of march." What could be better? Lions and tigers were added to the menagerie in 1925, and they prowled again in 1926. What a great idea! Well …

★ **Two constants through the years have been Santa's float, occasionally with Snow Babies hitching a ride, and a Christmas Goose float, occasionally with Mother aboard. In recent years, the classics combined, as Santa's throne took on a goose motif.**

As it turned out, rather than being delighted by these beasts from the jungle (via the Central Park Zoo), some children were terrified by all the growling and roaring. Macy's officials certainly didn't want to scare kids away. But what to do? They turned to Sarg, already a proven enchanter of children young and old. Tony, they asked, is there anything that can replace the animals?

The first four balloons, all designed by Sarg, appeared in the 1927 parade, and though they never got airborne—they were, in fact, oversized air-filled bags of rubber that were propped upright by handlers with sticks—they were an immediate smash. In 1928, Sarg designed a new series of rubberized-silk animal balloons that would be filled with helium. Supervising the construction, which took place at the Goodyear Tire & Rubber plant in Akron, Ohio, was an apprentice puppeteer named Bil Baird, who would go on to his own renown as a TV star and designer of the "Lonely Goatherd" marionette show in the film version of *The Sound of Music*. One of the Sarg-Baird balloons, a 125-foot-long dragon, required 50 wranglers to operate and created a great sensation. By 1929 the dragon had grown to 168 feet and was stealing headlines from Santa. "EVEN THE DRAGONS FEEL THE LURE OF THE GREAT WHITE WAY," said the *Daily News*, while the *American* pumped up the volume: "TERRIBLE FLYING DRAGON INVADES BROADWAY."

The early years of the balloons can best be described as rollicking. It took organizers a while to dial in the precise ratio of air to helium, and on more than one occasion a Macy's employee who had volunteered for duty as a balloon handler saw the parade from 10 feet above the street as he was yanked into the air by his flighty consort. Squeezing the balloons beneath elevated subways was always a nifty trick, and so was keeping them aloft; taxicabs with helium tanks chased the parade down Broadway. For a spectacular send-off at parade's end, it was decided to release the balloons on 34th Street and watch them float away. Wonderful notion, but no one remembered that helium expands with altitude, and one by one the 1928 balloons exploded before reaching the top of the department store. In 1929 safety valves were added to the 10 balloons, and the behemoths soared away, each of them tagged with Macy's address and the offer of a $25 reward for their

★**A 35-foot-long carnivorous fish swam downtown, "chased" by a rather timid 60-foot tiger. They were nearing the finish line at Macy's, whence they would be released into the wild blue yonder. The Empire State Building was still under construction in 1930 when high-flying Mrs. Katzenjammer bid the confines of New York adieu.**

return. Many were sent back from as distant as 100 miles, and many were returned riddled with bullet holes, indicating that word about the bounty had spread. One year the big dachshund landed in the East River and was torn apart by two warring tugboats. No reward was tendered. In 1931 the noted aviator Clarence Chamberlin was soaring over Brooklyn's Prospect Park when he

spotted a great pig off his wing. Impressing—or terrifying—his passengers, he deftly hooked his porcine quarry with a tow rope and brought home the bacon.

All this merriment was bound to come to an end, as the skies were getting more crowded each year. In 1932 a novice flyer was over nearby Jamaica Bay when she espied a giant cat. Having perhaps heard of Chamberlin's derring-do, she ignored her instructor's direction and headed straight at it. There was a collision, and while the puss got the worst of it, the plane's engine stalled. The good news is, the young lady regained control and landed safely. The bad news is, the incident wrote finis to releasing the balloons.

In a way, though, this was all for the best, as

Macy's made amends for its diminished climax by once again enlarging the parade—indeed, doubling its size. The 10th parade was the most enthusiastically received to date, with the crowds delighted by Macy's latest special effect: sound. The big baby balloon cried, the pig oinked, the dachshund barked, Andy the Alligator hissed malevolently (the noise created by frying bacon, amplified). A million spectators cheered this 1933 edition, which was recorded for newsreels and subsequently shown in theaters around the world. Tony Sarg was becoming famous beyond the canyons of New York, and in 1934 none other than Walt Disney was happy to collaborate with the puppeteer. The two men designed not only the first Mickey Mouse balloon but also a Horace Horse Collar, a Big Bad Wolf, an Oswald the Rabbit and a Pluto the Pup.

Another special partnership was forged in 1938 when WOR radio began broadcasting the parade live from Herald Square. The announcers didn't just call the floats and gasp at the balloons. There was real entertainment. For instance, Har-

po Marx coaxed laughs from the Depression-era audience in 1935.

The parade had it all figured out by 1941: It had stars, bands, fabulous floats and buoyant balloons. On what *The New York Times* called "one of the best days it has ever drawn in the weather lottery," the parade played to a million "amused and excited onlookers, a large part of them small fry … Fathers who probably hadn't lifted anything heavier than a drumstick or a cocktail for twelve months puffed and groaned as the small fry clambered over them, mishandling hats, noses, ears, hair and neckties, squealing in delight at the balloons and floats and cavorting clowns." Back at Macy's, Santa Claus shouted "Merry Christmas to you all!" and Dinah Shore sang a song commissioned for the occasion: "A Merry American Christmas." If there was one ominous note to the day, it was that the Santa Claus balloon, which was to lead a procession of seven, collapsed far uptown, "and had to be carted off ignominiously in a truck, a mere rubbery shadow of his hearty self."

Ten days after the joy of Thanksgiving had sub-

★ The first of three different Superman balloons to appear in the parade through the years enjoyed a commanding view of Times Square in 1940. An interesting footnote: In an earlier era, the balloons were sometimes recycled as different characters. This particular gasbag once came painted as a football player.

sided, Pearl Harbor erupted in explosion and the country was thrust into war. The 1942 news item in the *Times* concerning Macy's had a much different message: "The huge rubber dragon and six other giant balloons that were marched down Broadway last year in the Macy Thanksgiving parade were donated to the government's rubber scrap heap yesterday in ceremonies held on the steps of City Hall.

"In presenting the balloons to Mayor La Guardia, Jack I. Straus, president of Macy's, announced that the department store would not hold its Thanksgiving parade this year because it would require the services of 3,000 policemen and would involve a waste of rubber and gasoline …

Mr. Straus told the Mayor that it had been difficult to make a decision to eliminate the parade this year because of its popularity as a prelude to Christmas … 'Many graver sacrifices are being made by every one of us today,' he continued. 'We agreed that New Yorkers would understand and sympathize with the motives that prompted our decision and look forward as eagerly as we do to the time when the parade can again be resumed.'"

The parade was dark for three years. Those Thanksgiving mornings in 1942, '43 and '44 were given over to reflection and prayer, hardly to celebration. The holiday, thereby, lost some of its

essential character—its very reason for being.

Thanksgiving was not invented in 1621 by the Pilgrims of Plymouth, Massachusetts. It was invented both much earlier and, in the formal sense that we know it in America, much later than that. It was certified in this country by none other than Abraham Lincoln.

A bit of history gives perspective. The ancient Greeks used to offer thanks at harvest time to Demeter, goddess of the harvest, and the Romans similarly thanked Ceres, the goddess of corn. Harvest Home was an annual Anglo-Saxon feast day, and in Europe in the Middle Ages villagers attended church on Martinmas morning and communally shared roast goose in the afternoon, thanking St. Martin of Tours for their plenty.

America's Pilgrims did indeed invite Indians to their harvest festival in gratitude for help during that first brutal year, but those Puritans didn't consider such celebratory occasions to be akin to the far more solemn way they gave thanks to God. The Dutch who came later followed their homage to God with feasting, and traditions began to blend and evolve. During the Revolution, several days of thanksgiving were called by the Continental Congress to shore up spirits, and in 1789 George Washington proclaimed a national day of thanks on November 26.

Succeeding generations of New Englanders, meantime, had taken to celebrating each autumn's harvest in a traditional way: church, some manner of charity, a turkey-shooting contest, a sumptuous feast. When folks went westward, they took their customs along with them, and in 1844, Iowans gave thanks for a bumper crop, and three years after that San Franciscans did the same. All these rituals were part of the cultural record when, on October 3, 1863, President Lincoln recalled the recent battle of Gettysburg and the original Pilgrims, asking his countrymen "in every part of the United States, and also those who are at sea and those who are sojourning in foreign lands, to set apart and observe the last Thursday of November next as a day of thanksgiving and praise to our beneficent Father who dwelleth in the heavens."

From that day to this, perhaps no Thursday in November has ever more forcefully combined elemental thanks, relief and joy than November 22, 1945. The parade resumed with great spirit only weeks after the war had ended. An estimated 2 million spectators lined the route and caught a glimpse of the new America. Seven balloons? Let's have nine! Radio? Let's do TV! The first broadcast was carried only locally, but it spoke of the future, a

future that would transform and somehow enlarge everything in the country, including this parade. In 1947, Kansas City and Carson City and Kauai learned of the pageant when the hit movie *Miracle on 34th Street* brought news of it to theaters everywhere. In 1948, Boise and Branson and Billings saw it live when NBC took its telecast nationwide. Almost overnight, a strange locution was entering America's holiday lexicon, and America's great feast day was being co-opted. Instead of talking about "Macy's Christmas Parade" or, more correctly, "Macy's Thanksgiving Parade," people coast to coast were referring to "the Macy's Day Parade."

A third of the city was now turning out to see the parade annually. An ever-larger chunk of the country was watching each year from the living room. How not to disappoint all these people?

In the ethos of postwar America, the answer was obvious: more, more, more; better, better, better; bigger, bigger, bigger; louder, Louder, LOUDER! Bring on the stars! Milton Berle, the biggest thing in television, was Grand Marshal of the 1949 parade. The balloons burgeoned to enormous size and proliferated in number: 9, 10, 11. The floats grew not only in length but also in aspiration and—praise be—elegance. It was Macy's great good fortune to have the painter, sculptor and set designer Louis Kennel in its employ during the 1940s and '50s, and his floats have come to be regarded, along with the more modern models of Manfred Bass, as the creative equivalents of Tony Sarg's balloons. Bass, who designed for the parade from 1960 through the year 2000, said succinctly of Kennel: "He could make a brush sing."

He certainly made the parade sing, as did Jimmy Durante, Martha Raye and Eddie Fisher (garbed as Prince Charming in 1953). Danny Kaye, accompanied by daughter Dena, was Grand Marshal of

Hal Mathewson/
New York Daily News

Washington to ask Macy's—routinely the country's second-greatest consumer of helium, after the government itself—to go light on the gas. Light, as in oxygen. Macy's solution: Fill the balloons with air, hoist them on cranes and let the show go on.

And on and on. By the 1960s the Macy's Day Parade was old, venerable and—let's face it—rather routine. The 1960 parade was presided over by Bob Hope and broadcast in color for the first time, but these were enhancements, not major changes. The 1963 parade promised to be something different. New York City was to host a grand World's Fair the following year, and it was decided that the Macy's Day Parade would use this as a theme. It would beckon the nation to Queens!

And then …

On November 22, in Dallas, John F. Kennedy was assassinated. Macy's president Dave Yunich huddled with his troops, receiving counsel. Finally, he announced that the parade would be staged. "We feel it would be wrong to disappoint the millions of children throughout the country who look forward to this event each year with great anticipation," Yunich said. War had closed the parade, but the murder of a President did not. Still, the pageant that year had the feel of an Irish wake—forced revelry, some laughter, many tears. Every flag bore seven feet of black bunting. Lorne Greene and Betty White, serving as cohosts and beginning an association that would last 11 years, did their best to smile. But at day's end the country resumed its mourning.

Perhaps the shock of '63 was what the parade needed. Or perhaps it was the growing influence of gifted float designer Manny Bass. Or maybe it was Underdog's arrival as the 85th balloon in the parade's history in 1965. Or maybe it was the several appearances of Soupy Sales, along with guest spots by other icons of the era, such as Paul Anka, Alan King, Victor Borge, Fess Parker and, hardly least, the Munsters. Whatever it was, something juiced the parade throughout the remainder of the '60s, made it step livelier and look lovelier.

It was probably Bass more than anything. A native of Irvington, New Jersey, he had attended

★ **In 1955 the *Daily News* caption had some sport with this Thanksgiving gobbler: "Turkey is stuffed with helium." Ha, ha! Rain had been predicted, but when the day dawned bright and sunny, a massive crowd of 2,250,000 jammed the sidewalks. Opposite: One of New York's Finest Horses wasn't spooked by the Rocket Man.**

the 1955 parade, and other A-list stars during the Eisenhower years included Steve Allen, Sid Caesar, Connie Francis, Basil Rathbone (as Scrooge), Ginger Rogers, the Rockettes and, in saddle in different years, Roy Rogers and Hopalong Cassidy.

For all the wattage that the famous parade supplied, it was the simple pleasures that the spectators most enjoyed. Kaye would have been the first to admit that he was thoroughly upstaged in '55 by "the world's largest birthday cake," which rode aboard the Birthday in Tootsieland float. The cake's sole candle was a huge Tootsie Roll, from which leapt an acetylene-torch flame.

You can trot out the names and the flames, but you can't do a thing about the weather. In 1956 and 1957, it stunk. Forty-five-mile-an-hour winds howled in '56, wreaking havoc with the balloons, carving up Gobbler the Turkey, among others. In '57, Popeye's timbers were shivered by torrential rains during his first appearance. The next year, the sky was clear, but the air was still a problem. A severe nationwide helium shortage prompted

the Phoenix School of Design in New York City before being drafted into the Army. He joined Macy's after his discharge in 1960 and eventually oversaw all float construction in the store's Special Productions Studio. Working year-round and supervising 20 or more craftsmen, he built massive "traveling stages" for entertainers and their retinues. His creations were painstakingly detailed yet also overwhelming in their size and performance, as powerful hydraulics made dogs wag their tails and birds take flight. Bass modernized the parade, but with a classic sense of style that would have made Tony Sarg proud.

The parade, as with any long-running enterprise, was in need of another jump-start by the mid-1970s, and in 1977 Bass was presented with a dream collaborator in the person of Jean McFaddin, the new parade director. Manny and the Parade Lady would be a team until each retired after the 2000 event, and they would preside over a golden era of ever greater design, entertainment, innovation and, not coincidentally, television rat-

★ **From the *Post*, November 26, 1965: "Little Lynn Miller of Dayton, Ohio, struts like a trooper as she leads the Blackhawks band in Macy's Thanksgiving Parade. But then the marching gets to Lynn, as it might to any 5-year-old, and she pauses wearily."**

ings—an era marred only by one tragic occurrence that, when all was said and done, led to Macy's fashioning a safer if no less exciting parade for the new millennium.

★ ★ ★ ★ ★

The year 1977 was an interesting one for the parade. Well before Thanksgiving, Macy's was in the news when an auction of used floats and props at Christie's raised $75,000 for the Cystic Fibrosis Foundation. (Among the happy buyers was Texas billionaire Lamar Hunt, who walked away with the Humpty Dumpty and Rabbit floats, plus some Moppet heads, for a pittance: $6,120.) The auction can be seen in retrospect as a symbolic shedding of the old ways, particularly as it was simultaneous with the hiring of McFaddin, a Texan whose background was in the cutting-edge world of avant-garde theater. "I'll never forget my first parade," she said while reminiscing on the occasion of her retirement. "It was cold, but there was no sign of any weather. Then, at the big moment

when Santa Claus came into Herald Square, it started to snow. Big, fat flakes. It was beautiful. I knew that I had the best job on earth."

McFaddin loved Bass's work but felt Santa Claus needed an upgrade in accoutrement and status. She asked Manny to build Santa a new float, give him a new suit. And she determined that he would be restored to his original position of preeminence in the parade. "It's not that he was an afterthought," she said, "but with the balloons and everything else, somehow Santa and the kids had gotten lost a bit. This parade, when it's at its best, is about children. And Santa is about children. I wanted that focus."

In reestablishing a strong connection between the parade and Santa Claus, McFaddin was doing something as smart—and vital—as holding the

★ **Parade director McFaddin adjusted her topper in 1977— her first year— and conferred with colleague Tom Raney. Designer Bass hosted kids in 1998 in his Hoboken, New Jersey, studio just before one of his final parades.**

parade on Thanksgiving Day. By associating with Santa, Macy's was associating with the very best.

Who was he? Who was this Santa Claus? Kris Kringle? Who was this Saint Nicholas?

Let's start with Nicholas. He was a man born late in the 3rd century in Patara, which used to be a city in what is now Turkey. He was a devout and serious child who as a boy made a pilgrimage to Egypt and Palestine, seeking knowledge and enlightenment. He entered the nearby monastery of Sion and became a priest when he was only 19 years old. He was known as a very good, loving minister. He became Bishop of Myra in Lycia on the coast of what was then Asia Minor. There is a legend that he was imprisoned during Diocletian's persecution of Christians, then released under Constantine the Great—but much about this man who lived long ago is uncertain.

The often told tale regarding him goes like this: Nicholas came to know a poor man with three daughters, each of them personable, intelligent and altogether companionable. But no man would

★ **Whenever Santa arrived in New York to take part in the parade, he was treated royally by Macy's. Never had the great one's rig been so regal as in Bass's creation of a golden goose throne.**

marry any of the daughters because the father could not provide a dowry. The father grew saddened, the daughters despondent. Then, one December night, Nicholas passed the family's house. He threw three bags of money through an open window: the daughters' dowries. Each of the girls married, and the legend of Saint Nicholas as a charitable man and as a gift-giver was born.

After his death in the mid-300s, Nicholas was credited with many miracles. He was beatified, and came to be the patron saint of sailors, travelers, bakers, scholars, merchants and all of Russia—but primarily of children. He became famous, and by the Middle Ages, traditions were springing up that were associated with him. His feast day was celebrated in December, and in many European countries this became a day for celebration and exchanging presents.

Of the many places where Saint Nicholas was popular, he was most beloved in the Scandinavian countries and in Holland. The Dutch for "Saint Nicholas" is Sinterklaas, and when this name made its way to the English-speaking world, "Santa Claus" was born. (In other places, other names: Father Christmas, Père Noël, Kris Kringle.) In America, visions of Santa as rendered by 19th century writer Washington Irving and cartoonist Thomas Nast gave him shape. By the time the Macy's parade was born, we knew who Santa was.

And he was a soul well deserving of being Macy's Lord of the Dance. McFaddin put the spotlight back on Santa in 1978, then wondered where else she might shine it.

The short of it is, she simply let the parade be a parade, running from 77th Street down to 34th, and meanwhile turned Herald Square into an outdoor television studio. The Rockettes were joined on the makeshift stage not only by singers, bands and other dancers but by the casts of Broadway shows. In the living room, the Macy's Day Parade no longer looked like just a trundle of balloons—Ed McMahon saying, "There goes Donald Duck, here comes Mickey Mouse"—but like one of the snazziest shows on earth. Ratings rose like the huge new Superman balloon in 1980, and that year Macy's and NBC shared an Emmy award for their joint production. When Goodyear got out of the balloonmaking business in 1981, its decision coincided nicely with Macy's plans to bring more

★Santa Claus needed no help with his image, and his participation in the parade, truth be told, did nothing to increase his fame. In other instances, the Macy's parade has shown a remarkable capacity to lift a character's fortunes. The Cabbage Patch craze was fueled by a float, and such as Underdog and Spider-Man became nearly as well known for their synthetic incarnations as for their pen-and-ink versions.

Top Two: Goodyear/University of Akron, Anthony Casale/New York Daily News. Bottom Two: Thomas A. Kelly/Corbis, Reuters NewMedia/Corbis

★ Snoopy's roles: aviator in 1968 (top); astronaut in '73; flier, again, in '82; skater in '87 (left) and again in '95; millennium celebrant in 1999.

and more of the parade in-house. McFaddin contracted with Aerostar to help build new, Macy's-designed, urethane-coated nylon balloons. Spider-Man was a big hit, and so was Santa Goofy. In 1994, two instantly popular balloons were introduced, Barney the dinosaur and the Cat in the Hat. Three years later, Dr. Seuss's Cat would be involved in havoc unlike any the parade had seen.

On Thanksgiving morning, 1997, high winds made it difficult for handlers to control the balloons. Down Central Park West came the Cat, topped by its 18-foot-high red-and-white-striped hat. A sudden gust blew it into a lamppost, and a 100-pound cast-iron extension broke off. Moments earlier, New York City resident Kathy Caronna had handed her child to her husband. Good thing. The debris hit Caronna, fracturing her skull. After recovering from a monthlong coma, Caronna sued Macy's and the city of New York. She reached a settlement with both parties in 2001.

Even before the court action was drawing toward its conclusion, the incident, certainly the most tragic in the parade's history, had an effect on the event: A task force came up with recommendations to make the parade still safer. Balloon size was limited to 70 feet high, 78 feet long and 40 feet wide. As a result, the Pink Panther and Woody Woodpecker were retired. It was also decided that balloons would be grounded on any future Thanksgiving if sustained winds exceeded 23 miles per hour, or if gusts were above 34 mph. Beginning in 1998, all balloons were escorted not just by guides but also technicians carrying hand-held anemometers, along with police officers who had the authority to bring down any flier that seemed to pose a threat to public safety. It was ordered that light poles must not extend over the street, and further mandated that the airspace between a balloon and the street below not exceed one story. This is the good legacy to the parade, and to parade-goers, that the Cat in the Hat incident bequeathed.

More than two dozen big and small balloons, 21 floats, six "toy floats," seven falloons—hybrid floats topped by attached balloons—12 marching bands and 38 clown units marched in the 1998 parade. The parade, in other words, bounced right back. The crowds came back to the streets of New York. The audience came back to the telecast.

The Macy's Day Parade closed out the old millennium and plunged into the new in fine fashion, with delightful weather and a return to buoyancy. Spider-Man, Garfield and Underdog were out, but Blue, Arthur and Clifford were in. There was still a Turkey float, and Claus still presided, perhaps more authoritatively than ever. Jean McFaddin and Manny Bass retired, but successors brought renewed vigor to the cause. The 2001 event, the 75th running, was designed, in part by Bass protégé John Piper and balloon whiz Jimmy Artle, to represent a grand harmony of old and new. Curious George headed a cast of five rookie balloons, the largest freshman class in parade history, which brought the total of giants to 15; meantime, Big Bird returned and Mark Schonberg, who had called every parade since 1975 from his uptown platform, limbered up his vocal cords. Carrying the load—manning the floats, wearing the clowns' greasepaint—were gleeful folks from

★ **The parade goes on and on, and as long as it does, there will be a turkey, as there was in the year 2000. It's a safe bet that there will also be dogs. The Pets.com sock puppet was represented by a falloon in 1999, and Federated Department Stores' greendog rode one in 2000 (below). How many more and different Snoopys we will get to see is anyone's guess.**

Macy's cosmetics department, ladies' furnishings, boardroom and stockroom. Just as in 1924.

Herbert Straus long ago promised New York a surprise it would never forget. Macy's delivered for the city then, and continues to deliver for the country each Thanksgiving morning. America pauses on that festive and solemn day to give thanks for many large and small blessings. One of them is the parade—their parade, the country's parade, America's parade. A parade of many fun, surprising, colorful images.

Now, on with the images. Let's have a parade!

First Steps

In the Roaring Twenties and desperate thirties, the parade found its feet—and made its way to the heart of New York.

1924–1941

The first was as much party as parade, an affirmative response to a large and impassioned group of employees who had petitioned for their right to frolic in the streets. Only two blocks long in 1924, the Christmas Parade, as it was then called, was clearly a brilliant idea from the get-go, an overnight sensation, an instant institution. Careering through its early years with one wacky experiment after another—leading to all those exploding balloons, barking balloons, spectacular effects and spectacular accidents—the parade found itself, by the early '40s, famous. Then on November 27, 1941, in what now seems an eerily ominous happenstance, the Santa balloon blew up only 10 days before bombs fell on Pearl Harbor. The aftershocks of the attack in Hawaii shattered the country and shuttered the Macy's Day Parade, as it had by then become known, for three gray years.

As an early parade crossed Amsterdam Avenue, what would become staples were already in place: a band, a float and Santa Claus. There were, however, no balloons.

★ A Star Is Born

Ads trumpeted the inaugural event in 1924, and follow-up articles raved. "Starting with a bang, the parade of tableaux, comedians, tragedians, clowns, tumblers, camels ... began at 145th street and Convent avenue at 9 A.M.," reported the *Newark Ledger.* "[E]verybody caught the spirit of North Pole land at the first sight and sound of the Kris Kringle bands. They climbed everything there was to climb; they almost fell out of the tops of buses to see." Macy's red star logo, derived from a Nantucket whalers' symbol, hung from every horse.

★ **Kringle's Co-stars**
The big theme has always been Christmas; after all, it was initially called Macy's Christmas Parade, not Macy's Thanksgiving Day Parade. But some of the incarnations featured dominant subthemes like, for instance, the alphabet. At the first parade in '24, only Santa Claus himself was billed above the equally immortal Mother Goose. Storybook floats transported the tub trio, Miss Muffet and the Old Lady who was at a loss.

MACY'S
CHRISTMAS PARADE
LITTLE MISS MUFFET

★ **Fairyfolk Frolics**

A 1924 account read: "A kid called out 'Three Cheers for Santa Claus' in a piping voice as the old gentleman arrived at the fairy window and spread his arms wide apart for all to view the fairy wonders." It was the climactic moment of a triumphant day when the shades were drawn up and people flooded 34th Street to peer at the animated scenes in Macy's windows.

**We Thank
The People of New York
And Adjacent Communities**

for the overwhelming interest and festive enthusiasm which helped us make yesterday's Christmas Parade such a magnificent spectacle. We did not dare to dream its success would be so great.

The day will linger long in the memories of the numberless thousands of youngsters who lined the six-mile route of march to welcome Santa Claus and his fantastic Wonderland retinue upon his entry to New York. And just as many grown-ups will cherish the memory.

The tremendous ovation which you accorded to yesterday's procession has led us to decide that, barring unforeseen obstacles,

such a parade will hereafter be an annual feature of Macy's Christmas program for the people. We advise you now to make no other engagements for the morning of Thanksgiving Day, 1925.

We don't know how many thousands of people saw the initial showing of "The Fairyfolk Frolics of Wondertown" yesterday—we were all too excited to count. But we are sure that such a tribute has never before been accorded to any window display anywhere in this country.

Macy's "Fairyfolk Frolics" will perform daily until Christmas from 9 a. m. to midnight in the famous 75-foot window on 34th Street, between 6th and 7th Avenues.

To-day, the schools being closed, is a good time to bring the children to see it.

Beginning to-day, and every day until Christmas, Santa Claus is in Wonderland on Macy's Fourth Floor, from 9 a. m. to 5:30 p. m., and will be glad to meet all the little folk who greeted him yesterday, and all other little children who behave themselves.

R. H. Macy & Co.
Inc.   NEW YORK CITY
34th ST. & BROADWAY

Animals borrowed from the Central Park Zoo marched in the parade from 1924 to 1926, though the giraffe had to stand aside lest he bump his head on the El.

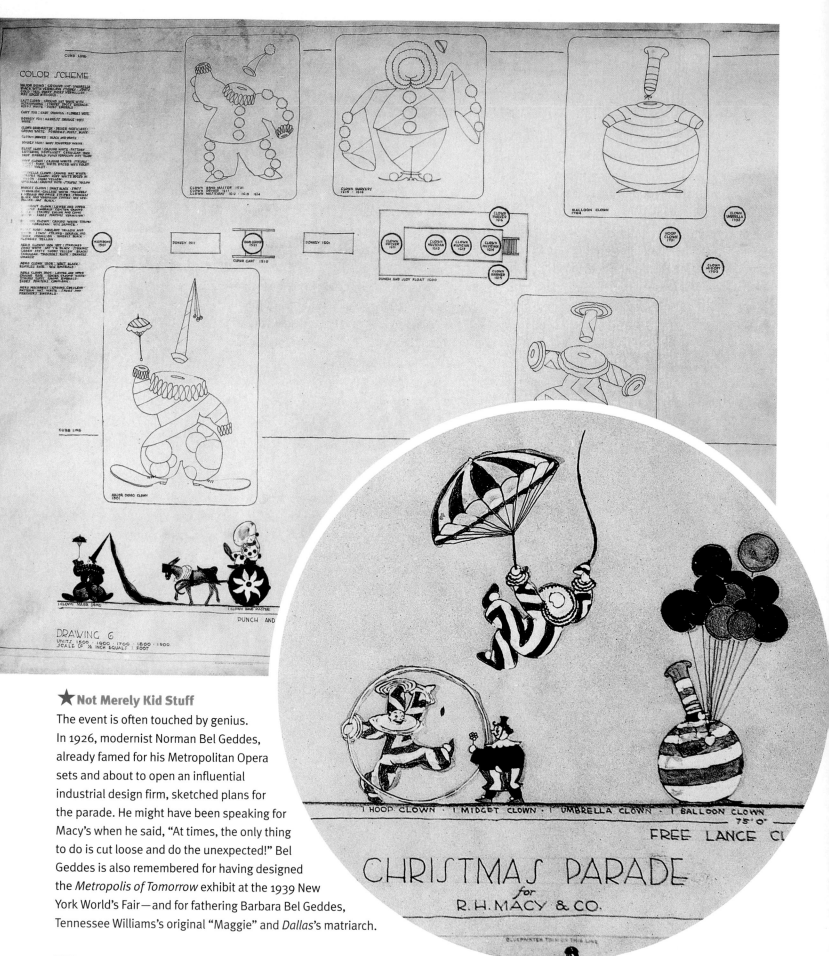

★ **Not Merely Kid Stuff**

The event is often touched by genius. In 1926, modernist Norman Bel Geddes, already famed for his Metropolitan Opera sets and about to open an influential industrial design firm, sketched plans for the parade. He might have been speaking for Macy's when he said, "At times, the only thing to do is cut loose and do the unexpected!" Bel Geddes is also remembered for having designed the *Metropolis of Tomorrow* exhibit at the 1939 New York World's Fair—and for fathering Barbara Bel Geddes, Tennessee Williams's original "Maggie" and *Dallas*'s matriarch.

My Dear Price:
I don't mind putting my name on this — but is it really essential that you hang it up in the office? Otherwise my best wishes!

Norman Bel Geddes

7 December 1926

★ The Party Within the Parade

In the beginning, the march down Broadway was equally to entertain the onlookers and, à la Mardi Gras, to provide merriment for the marchers themselves. In the prewar years, Macy's employees staffed all the floats and played nearly all the parts, such as devils, King Neptune—and pirates of both sexes. And the spectators were encouraged to fall in behind Santa.

★ Real Animals Yield to the Very, Very Unreal

When lions and tigers got the heave-ho in 1927, they were replaced not by replicas but by puffed-up phantasmagoria. Of the initial four balloons, three were thoroughly anonymous beasties—including a dragon that would get the occasional face-lift in the parade's early years—and one was a nationally famous personality: Felix the Cat (right), a big cartoon star since 1919. It's interesting to note that when Felix bowed, no fees were paid to Macy's; today it takes real money to get a trademarked character into the parade. The very first balloons were earthbound, air-filled puppets. Second-generation creations, including a new and improved Felix, took flight.

★ **The Party Before the Parade**

What would become a Big Apple tradition second only to the great event itself—trekking to the Upper West Side to watch the balloons inflate—started small. In 1929 neighborhood cops and kids watched one of the Katzenjammers and Lightning, a 40-foot horse, get their helium. The seriously misnamed Lightning then led 10 balloons downtown on a blustery day. At 90th Street a big rubber dog slipped a leash and was taken down, and at 58th a gust blew a turkey against a NO PARKING sign, causing a gash. In Herald Square all tethers were severed and the balloons flew yonder—except for Captain Katzenjammer. His heavy moustaches acted as ballast, and as *Time* reported, "Herr Inspektor, loath to soar, ogled into office windows until 20 feet had been cut off his traditional whiskers." Then he joined the family aloft.

★**Hard to Handle**
In the beginning there was trial and error. The very earliest balloons, like The Turk, at left, and Broadway Bill, opposite, often yanked their wranglers into the air when caught by a gust. The behemoths made their wobbly way through the canyons of midtown, bobbing and weaving. It was anyone's bet how many would make it to the finish line.

★ Dash Away, Dash Away, Dash Away, All!

As a bonus extravaganza from 1928 through 1932, balloons were released at parade's end. Most of their hides were later recovered in exchange for a reward. The best fliers traveled as far as 100 miles, and several came back clearly the worse for wear. Andy the Alligator was returned in two pieces one year; other critters had very evidently been shot down by bounty hunters. But if their landings were sometimes hard, their takeoffs were always spectacular—none more so than that of this 168-foot dragon in 1929, who strained to escape the masses in front of Macy's, then rose, liberated, over the elevated subway.

HERE'S TONY SARG'S *own* PICTURE *of the famous* THANKSGIVING DAY PARADE. STRAIGHT DOWN BROADWAY, NEW

YORK, *to the* GREATEST STORE *in the* WORLD, *the* FAMOUS MACY BALLOONS PARADED *to* WELCOME SANTA CLAUS *to*

MACY'S. MORE THAN 1 MILLION NEW YORKERS LINED *the* SIDEWALKS *and* WATCHED *and* LAUGHED *and* CHEERED.

★ **The Man Behind the Marvels**

His name was Tony Sarg, and he was the inventor of the Macy's Day Parade that America would come to know and love. An illustrator and puppeteer, the immigrant Sarg helped design the parade from the very beginning; he was also the artist behind Macy's fabulous window displays. His studio fashioned all the first balloons, including the much beloved dachshund, something of an earlier-era Underdog. In 1932, Sarg, a charismatic and debonair man who imbued the parade with his joyful spirit, crafted a puzzle that depicted the march down Broadway.

★ **Bringing Cheer to the Depression-Era Masses**

The pig was pleased in 1931 when, after being released at parade's end, he was snared by an aviator in the skies over Brooklyn and brought safely back to his Macy's pen. The bird was expressionless throughout the early '30s, but the baby howled during his trip through Times Square in '33; perhaps it was because he couldn't fit into the Criterion to take in the Noël Coward hit *Design for Living*.

Press accounts wore out the word.
Women's Wear Daily: "Grotesque
Beasts." The *Times:* "grotesque figures."
The *Sun* had it as a noun: "Grotesques."

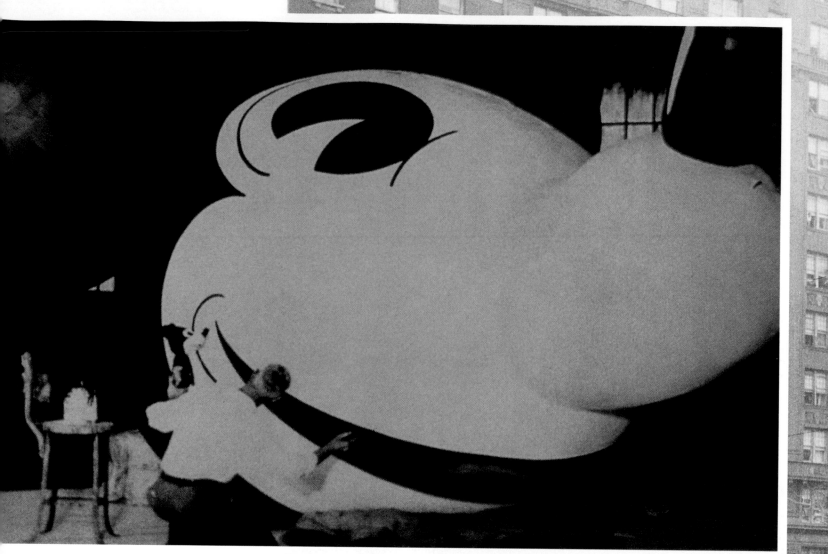

★ Hardly Mini Mickey

In 1934, two genius animators—Walt Disney and Macy's Tony Sarg—teamed up for the first of several Disney balloons that would float through the years. It was, of course, Mickey Mouse, star of *Steamboat Willie* (1928) and other cartoon classics. Sarg and Disney's fortunes diverged after their collaboration. Disney made America's first feature-length cartoon, *Snow White and the Seven Dwarfs,* in 1937 and was on his way to an empire. Sarg's business went bankrupt in 1939, and to settle his debts, he had to sell his puppets. Tony Sarg, the heart and soul of the Macy's parade, died in 1942 at age 60, after an emergency appendectomy.

Goodyear/University of Akron

★ **Echoes of Long-ago Bay State History in the Streets of New York**

In the mid-1800s, R.H. Macy, a native of Nantucket Island in Massachusetts, did what many Nantucket lads did: He served as a cabin boy aboard a whaler. A century later, in 1937, an homage to the department store's founder came in the form of the Nantucket Sensation Sea Dragon balloon, seen above at the Museum of Natural History. In 1621, elsewhere in Massachusetts—in Plymouth—Pilgrims broke bread with American Indians at a harvest celebration. On Thanksgiving Day, 1935, a balloon above Broadway commemorated the event.

★ The Giants Grow Ever More Gigantic

The parade spread its wings, taking to the air via radio station WOR in 1938, reaching beyond the one-million-plus spectators it was routinely drawing to the sidewalks of New York. The creed of The World's Largest Store had long held that bigger is better, which extended not only to the burgeoning parade but to the figures therein. The football player's head was eight feet six inches in diameter, and when set atop his body completed a fearsome 75-foot-high gridder. Filled with 9,000 cubic feet of helium, he dominated Central Park in 1941.

By the 1940s the immense parade—twice the size of earlier versions—was soaring, full of confidence, providing a glimmer of joy to millions just emerging from a long Depression.

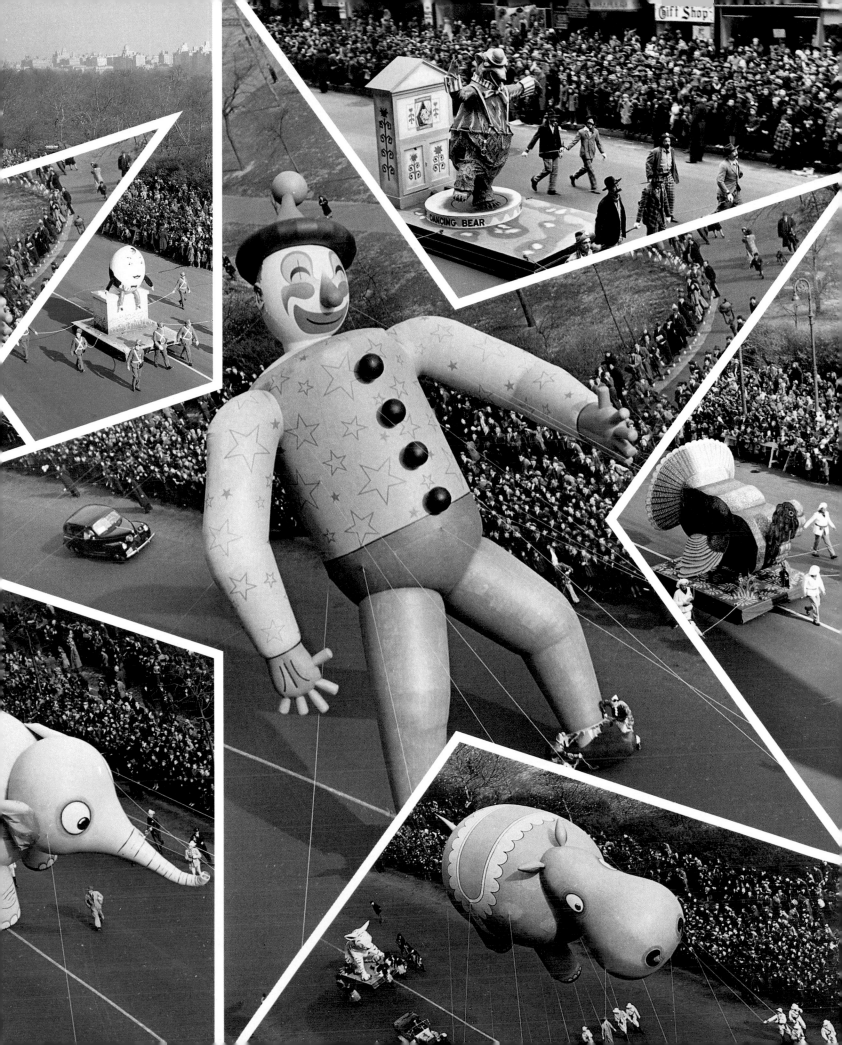

★ **Weegee's Parade**

From 1930 to 1947, the New York demimonde that would come to be known as the Naked City was chronicled by an extraordinary photographer wielding a Speed Graphic camera and, often, a Compur flash unit. The formal name of this immigrant son of a rabbi was Usher H. Fellig, but he was known professionally as Weegee. His unique eye made life after dark seem simultaneously surreal and all too real. He chased after lowlifes, celebrities and the frequent victims of Murder, Inc., recording what actually happened, filtered through the Weegeean sensibility. Perhaps no subject made Weegee's strange world seem more bizarre than a balloon being inflated on the eve of the big event.

Having recorded more than enough murdered mobsters, Weegee knew how to bring life to a body prone.
He traveled the nocturnal streets in his 1938 Chevrolet, looking for trouble or anything interesting. The trunk
of his car served as a darkroom, and photos taken between midnight and five a.m. might be in the evening
edition of the newspaper *PM*. He stamped the back of each print CREDIT PHOTO BY WEEGEE THE FAMOUS, and
he wasn't bragging. His first book, *Naked City,* inspired the 1948 movie, and Weegee had popped nationwide.

★ **Rubber Ploughshares into Swords**

As interventionists and isolationists dueled over what the United States should do about the war in Europe in the late 1930s, a wave of patriotism swept the land and the Uncle Sam balloon became a dominant image in the parade. While the 45-foot Santa—a popular subject for Weegee and other photographers of the late 1930s—floated along without incident for a few years, in 1941 he made it only 20 blocks before running out of gas (above). An omen, perhaps? Only days later, Japan's surprise attack on Pearl Harbor finally drew the U.S. into the battle it had long been resisting. The parade was halted as rubber and helium were needed for the war effort, specifically for dirigibles. In retrospect, the Macy's Thanksgiving Day Parade of '41 can be seen as America's last bright party before entering into four years of darkness.

Miracle of a Movie

★★ *To me, imagination is a place all by itself. A separate country. Now, you've heard of the French nation, the British nation—well, this is the imagination. A wonderful place.* ★★

— Kris Kringle, in *Miracle on 34th Street*

Valentine Davies worked in that "wonderful place."

This native New Yorker was, as World War II ended, a playwright and novelist entering his forties with not a lot on his résumé but with a lovely notion in his head. After the long, wearying years of war, he gazed at the balloons returning to Broadway and wondered: What would happen if Santa Claus visited our town at Christmastime?

Davies had, in recent years, tried his hand at Hollywood fare; he had received a story credit on the little-noticed 1942 film *Syncopation*. A friend of his was the noted screenwriter George Seaton, the adapter of *Charley's Aunt* and *The Song of Berna-*

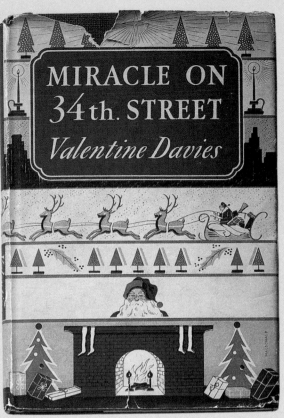

★ The talents of stars O'Hara and Payne, old Edmund Gwenn and young Natalie Wood—and, most important, wordsmith Valentine Davies— converged at a cosmically correct moment in 1947.

dette, who was just then turning to directing. Davies told Seaton of his what-if, and Seaton suggested in turn: What if it's not really an elf, but a guy who *thinks* he's Santa?

Seaton and Davies collaborated on the script for 18 months, usually working together a couple of nights a week. For Davies especially, the project was a passion. He thought up situations and dialogue for the screenplay, even as he simultaneously filed away paragraphs that would become a novella of his story. He wrote wherever he was. For a while he holed up at the Hidden Well guest ranch at the corner of Sunset and Paradise in Las Vegas, working on his urban Christmas tale under the hot desert sun. (If it's interesting that O. Henry wrote "The Gift of the Magi" in a corner booth at Pete's Tavern in lower Manhattan, it's perhaps even more so that another luminous seasonal story of a New York yuletide was partially crafted in Sin City.)

Davies and Seaton felt they were onto something big with *Miracle on 34th Street.* Not everyone agreed. Darryl Zanuck, the powerful head of 20th

★ The film gets off to a rip-snorting start when, at the parade, Kringle (left) scolds a drunk Santa. High above the hullabaloo and not particularly interested in the balloons, Susan meets her mom's new suitor, Mr. Gailey.

Century Fox, didn't want to make the film. But he did want Seaton to work on *Chicken Every Sunday,* a folksy vehicle that Zanuck saw as a sure winner. Seaton offered Zanuck a twofer—I'll do that if you do this—and *Miracle* got its green light. (A footnote: *Chicken Every Sunday,* also based on a Seaton-Valentine script, was a modest success in 1949.)

In the Christmas season of 1946, as Frank Capra's *It's a Wonderful Life* was eliciting tears from America's moviegoers, *Miracle* was being filmed on and near 34th Street. For 22 days, cameras and crew invaded Macy's, shooting in offices, hallways, locker rooms. They shot the parade, of course, and when final tallying was done, it turned out that more than half of the characters in the movie were played by Macy's employees.

The lead actors were hardly superstars but, rather, contract pros John Payne and Maureen O'Hara. Production notes prepared for the film's opening predicted that nine-year-old Natalie Wood's "interpretation of a sweet, but blasé city child will prove a great boost to the career of this newcomer." Maybe it would, but, frankly, there was no great buzz attendant upon the release of *Miracle.*

Not least, you might reason, since the producers, in their dubious wisdom, debuted the film not at Thanksgiving of 1947 but earlier, during the summer. It would take a miracle for the movie to last

that today seems remarkable, its buoyant comedy, its wholesome moral, and a slew of terrific performances. The leads are fine, and supporting them is one scene-stealer after another. Wood's character, a savvy little girl named Susan, could eat Madeline or Eloise for breakfast. And if any film stands as Exhibit A that the immediate postwar years continued a golden age of Hollywood character acting, it would be *Miracle on 34th Street*. Edmund Gwenn's Academy Award–winning performance as Kringle was the pinnacle of an 87-film career. ("Now I know there's a Santa Claus," said the 72-year-old actor upon receiving his Best Supporting Actor Oscar.) Gene Lockhart's turn as the beleaguered Judge Harper and William Frawley's as the judge's backstage political boss were just as sharp. Uncredited in her film debut, Thelma Ritter was hilarious.

For the reader who has been living under a rock

till Christmas, never mind into any kind of celluloid eternity. But that's the thing about miracles: They're out of our hands.

Kate Cameron of the *Daily News* dutifully made her way to the Roxy in the dog days of '47 expecting not much. She was as surprised as anyone when her review read, "Of course, there's a Santa Claus, and I have been too stupid not to have had a sustained faith in the jolly old fellow." She saw the film as not merely funny but "something more, with an undefinable spiritual quality that raises the spirits of the beholder in a happy, hopeful mood." She gave it four stars.

As the holidays neared, the lines lengthened at the Roxy; six months after opening, the movie was, amazingly, still running daily. By Thanksgiving, Payne and O'Hara were stars in a higher firmament, and Macy's, for its part, was smart enough to see—just as the Macy's in the movie had—that it was being given a unique marketing opportunity. The handsome O'Hara and Payne were invited to greet the annual parade at Times Square, and they happily assented. The store was happy, Zanuck was happy, Seaton was happy and Valentine Davies, whose book version was selling copies even as his film was filling seats, was very, very happy.

Is *Miracle on 34th Street* really that good?

Absolutely. An often sentimental film, it is redeemed by its constant charm, a sophistication

★ **Kringle and Gailey have found their way into the Walkers' home. But the big question is: How to capture their hearts?**

this last half century, a synopsis of what *Miracle* is about and why it works so well: An elderly gent named Kris Kringle (Gwenn) is hired by Doris Walker, a hard-headed Macy's employee (O'Hara), to play Santa in the parade and in the store. The wrinkle is, Kringle insists he really is Santa, and behaves as Santa might. He has a generosity of spirit so large that he begins advising customers to shop elsewhere for toys they can't find at Macy's. Even as Mr. Macy begins to realize that Kris's benevolence reflects well upon his store, another Macy's employee, played with a divine sleaziness by Porter Hall, seeks to have Kringle committed as insane.

Fred Gailey (Payne) is a lawyer who has eyes for Doris but does not understand her cynicism or why she has willfully infected her

★ **Kringle's whiskers are real all right, but that's not enough to convince little Susan of Santa's existence.**

daughter, Susan, with an anti-Santa virus. Gailey sets out to win over both Doris and Susan by proving in court that not only is there a Santa Claus, but that he is the fellow who works at Macy's. The denouement, involving U.S. government complicity in the Santa saga, is one of the finest in movie history, and the viewer is left repeating along with Susan the mantra "I believe." Yes, the film is manipulative—it was released in England as *The Big Heart,* which surely is what a romanticized British movie about Harrods' Father Christmas would be called in the States—but it is never false, a surpassing accomplishment for a fantasy.

★ **Susan, falling under Kris's spell, monkeys around (opposite). Above: The crucial evidence is presented. In the remake, the "proof" didn't have to do with letters to Santa but with the IN GOD WE TRUST slogan on legal tender, pointing up only too well the difference between 1947 America and the 1990s version.**

The movie was perfect for a postwar audience needing to smile, and for the subsequent generation of baby boomers who watched on television. For them, Christmas was the biggest of big deals, and their parents were happy to expose them to a story that boosted the values of kindness, honesty, faith—and that was, at bottom, a critique of commercialization. Ahead of its time in many ways (Doris was a divorced single mom with a job; Kris suffered a trial for lunacy), the movie has never become dated. It remains as huge today—a 1997 poll said 82 percent of Americans have seen it and 55 percent have watched it five or more times—as it was when it first opened.

And at the time, it was a smash. Seaton and Davies won Oscars for their writing, though the film was beaten for Best Picture by *Gentleman's Agreement*. As with anything so successful, there were several quick attempts to reinterpret it, reinvent it,

recapture its magic. In December 1947 and again in '48, Payne, O'Hara and Gwenn gathered in a radio studio to do a live one-hour version of *Miracle* for the Lux Radio Theatre. Scores of plays based on the script, often bolstered by material from Davies's book, have been staged through the years by regional theaters, and in 1963 *Music Man* Meredith Willson wrote the book, music and lyrics for a Broadway version. *Here's Love* lasted 334 performances but is remembered as mediocre. It is notable as a big-budget show about Christmas that contributed not a single standard to the Yule canon. (When was the last time you sang "Big Ca-lown Balloons" or "The Plastic Alligator" by the hearth?)

As if annual showings of the original weren't enough, *Miracle on 34th Street* was remade as a television movie thrice over, with actors such as Sebastian Cabot and Ed Wynn failing to challenge Gwenn's definitive Kringle. Inevitably, it was remade

as a feature film, too. In 1994, Sir Richard Attenborough was an effective Santa in a *Miracle on 34th Street* that was, ultimately, not a patch on the original. Screenwriter John Hughes—he of *Home Alone*—eschewed slyness and subtlety in favor of hammering his audience over the head, pumping up the volume and the schmaltz. In reshaping *Miracle*'s gemlike ending, he substituted a blatant religiosity for Davies's blithe spirituality. When buying your DVD, reach for the original (preferably not the colorized version).

While Seaton went on to direct successful films ranging from *The Country Girl* to *Airport*, O'Hara enjoyed a fine career and Wood became a high-wattage star, it is fair to say that participation in *Miracle on 34th Street* was a high point for all involved. In 1991, O'Hara, appearing on Johnny

Carson's *Tonight Show*, told the story of coming from Mass in New York City only days earlier. Two little boys followed her and finally summoned the courage to tug on her coat. "Are you the lady that knows Santa Claus?" one asked. "Yes, I know him well," O'Hara replied. She told Carson: "A hundred years from now, long after I'm nailed into the box, you'll still be seeing Maureen O'Hara in *Miracle on 34th Street* every Christmas and *The Quiet Man* on Saint Paddy's Day."

As we view *Miracle* a century on, we'll still be wondering at its magic. Valentine Davies died in 1961 after a successful screenwriting career that never saw him again find quite the same place in that separate country, that wonderful place, the imagination. But he found it once.

It was a miracle, somehow out of his hands.

★ A pocketful of *Miracles:* The film remake (above and right) was careful not to implicate Macy's, changing the store's name to Cole's. In the Payne role, rising star Dylan McDermott got some acting practice for *The Practice. Here's Love* (below, left) was musical but not lyrical. On TV, neither Wynn (center) nor Cabot (right) made us forget Gwenn.

America's Parade

1945–1963

A New York City tradition went nationwide, riding the airwaves into the country's homes, where the baby boom generation was waiting eagerly at the tube.

The country was awash in relief, joy and—not least—pride in 1945. And the revived Macy's Thanksgiving Day Parade was well positioned to reflect America's mood, as it had always been an emotional, boisterous, even triumphal affair. However, it had been, prewar, essentially a New York institution—the private little secret of a million city dwellers and suburbanites who ventured into the cold, and a few million more who listened by the hearth. *Miracle on 34th Street* began to change things. The movie whetted America's appetite for a better view of the proceedings, and there was clearly only one way to satisfy the craving. Television and the parade were a fine fit from the onset, and before long the American Christmas season had fixed parameters: Opens with Macy's Day Parade on Thanksgiving Morning … Culminates with Santa's Visit. In between—Shopping!

Times Square, even more than the Mall in Washington, was the nation's commons in '45. People danced in the streets to celebrate victory in Europe, and again for victory over Japan. On Thanksgiving morning, more joy.

Keystone/Gamma

★ Back in Action

Flush with victory, Americans turned out to celebrate—and to give thanks—on Thanksgiving morning, 1945, as a giant teddy bear, one of nine new balloons, made his way serenely through Times Square, passing the Statue of Liberty model that had been a centerpiece of V-E and V-J Day festivities earlier in the year. Men and women from the armed services were properly honored, and their military transport, including this amphibious craft, did some light lifting for a change—escorting such as ice-cream cones, rather than hitting beaches with violent intent.

★ **The Start of Something Big**

In 1945, NBC trained its cameras on the parade for the first time, sending images that included an animal act—not to mention the smoking sailor in the famous Camel live-action billboard—to folks throughout the greater New York viewing area. (The peacock network would stay with the parade through the years, as a procession of *Today Show* hosts, beginning with Dave Garroway in 1953, took over the commentary.) When the broadcast went nationwide in 1948, only one year after *Miracle on 34th Street* had introduced Macy's big event to moviegoers from Maine to Miami, D.C. to L.A., the Thanksgiving extravaganza became a part of the seasonal fabric. It became America's Parade.

★ In Living Color

Television in no way lessened
the crowds, as the tube simply couldn't
convey the excitement of being there. Two million
attended in 1945; Dad boosted this young one to a better view in Times Square
in 1947; barriers held back throngs in 1948. A large attraction was big-name
stars. Milton Berle, "Mr. Television," was Grand Marshal of the 1949 parade, a
year that also featured the debut of marionette Howdy Doody, whose fame
rivaled even Uncle Miltie's. Once, when Howdy and his human sidekick Buffalo
Bob appeared at Macy's, they set off a stampede for 10,000 Doody dolls.

In the late 1940s, new characters were added to the roster. This clown bowed in 1945: It would be recycled as a ballplayer, policeman and fireman. A pirate (né a Pilgrim) boarded in '48, as *Joan of Arc*, starring Ingrid Bergman, burned up the box office.

The latest in Macy's long and noble line of dachshunds takes a turn through Times Square in 1953, then scampers the final blocks to 34th Street.

★ He's Popeye the Sailor Man

Popeye was created in January 1929 by cartoonist Elzie Segar and recreated in 1957 by engineer William Ludwick and draftsman Jack Grisak of Goodyear Tire & Rubber's Aviation Products Division. Segar's Popeye was a 34-year-old serviceman who stood five foot six and weighed 154 pounds. Goodyear pumped him up tenfold, to 56 feet, filling him with helium rather than spinach. Once assembled in Akron, Popeye was test-flown at the airfield. All seemed A-O.K., but rain during the parade collected in Popeye's cap, causing his 14-foot head to dip, then snap back to attention.

★ Building a Better—Or At Least Bigger—Bullwinkle

In the 1950s, animator Jay Ward concocted a delightfully subversive cartoon starring Bullwinkle J. Moose and Rocket J. Squirrel who fought battles with Boris Badenov and Natasha Fatale to keep the world safe for … well, for mooses, squirrels and the American way of life. By 1961, Bullwinkle was sufficiently famous to be floated in the parade, an affirmation for a cartoon character equivalent to an actor's getting cement prints outside Grauman's Chinese Theatre. On the floor of the Goodyear plant, the 65-foot-tall balloon took shape, then received a final bit of polishing. Bullwinkle proved a popular creation: By the mid-1990s, he was the Thanksgiving pageant's oldest returning veteran.

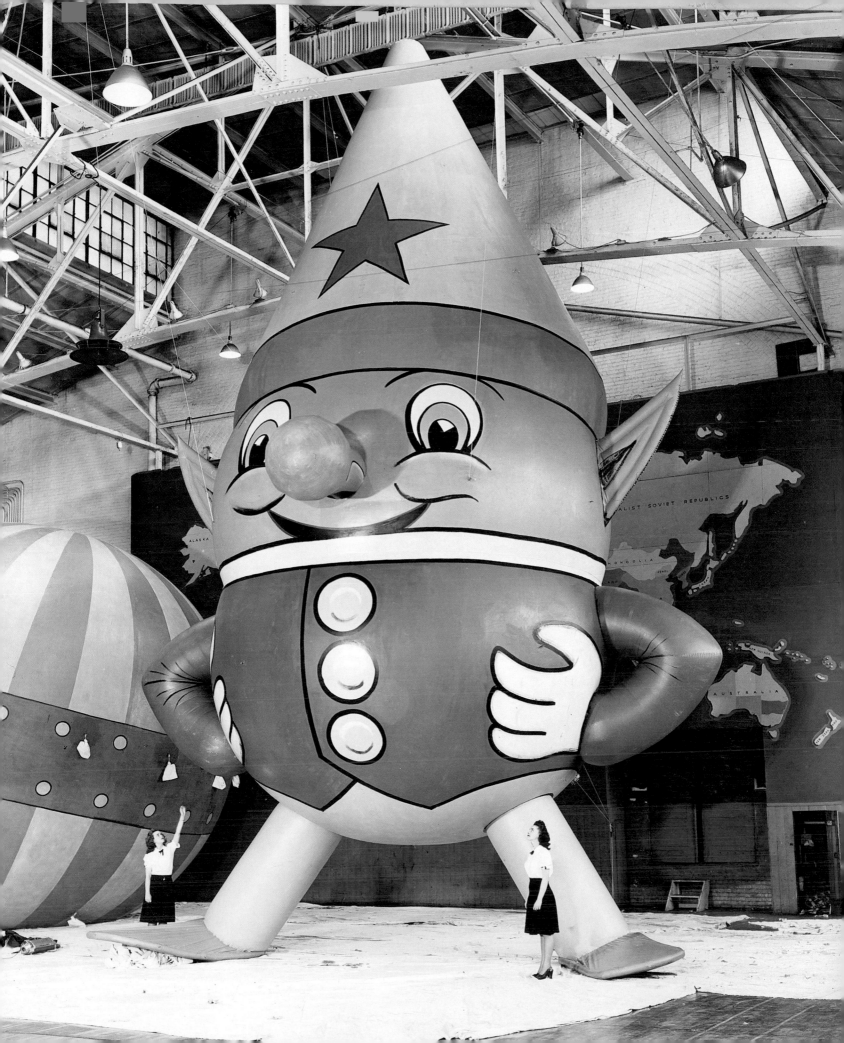

As impressive as the balloons appeared when aloft, they seemed even more awesome when inflated indoors, as this porky pig, plus the happy clown and goofy gnome on the previous pages, prove.

★ **Unable to Fly, Unable to Float**

In 1956, Mighty Mouse set forth on what would be a tumultuous journey to Herald Square. Battered by 45-mile-an-hour gusts before he reached Columbus Circle, he was brought to his knees. His reputation at stake—"Here I come to save the day!"—the game rodent struggled on to Macy's before collapsing in a heap. Gobbler, a big turkey, came a-cropper in the wind, as did a Civil War–themed balloon called Observer. In 1958, responding to a national helium shortage, the U.S. government asked Macy's to forgo its usual gas consumption. Air-filled balloons were chauffered south by trucks with cranes (opposite).

Hal Mathewson/New York Daily News (2)

Frank Hurley/New York Daily News

★ **There's Much More Than Merely Those Big Rubber Things**

With their introduction in the late 1920s, balloons quickly became the signature attraction of the parade. But even before the idea of balloons was floated, there were the floats. In 1959 the Story Book float (left) was helmed by former child star Shirley Temple Black, while elsewhere the Rockettes rode the Music Hall float and Connie Francis was borne down Broadway on the Cinderella float. And then there are the high school marching bands, like the one leading Popeye. Macy's receives videotapes from hundreds of them annually, each hoping to be among the dozen or so to make the final cut. Bake sales and car washes are staged nationwide to send the lucky Sousa-playing winners to New York City.

★ The Floatmeister

The storied Tony Sarg was renowned for his balloons. In the postwar years, the lord of the floats—the Sarg of Macy's earthbound extravaganzas—was stage-set designer Louis Kennel. Born in 1886, he worked out of his studio in Secaucus, New Jersey. There, in the late '40s and early '50s, he applied finishing touches to dozens of reindeer, designed the popular cow-over-the-moon set piece and crafted an Indian head that greatly impressed a neighborhood lad. In the 1949 parade, Cow, one of 16 floats, was manned by TV star Paul Winchell.

★ **The Birth of a Cow**

From scale models to plaster casts to finishing touches, the assembly of Elsie the Cow proceeded in stages that can be seen in these disquieting, Daliesque images. Elsie had debuted at the New York World's Fair of 1939. In the 1963 parade she was

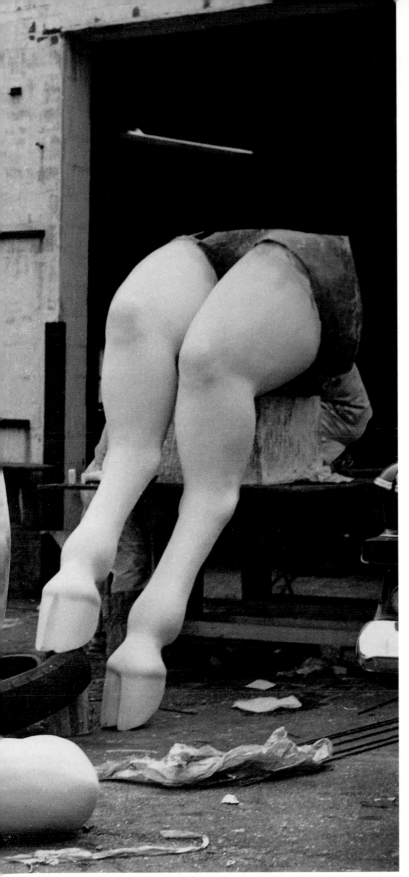

heralding the city's 1964 exposition, to open shortly in Queens. She was also, of course, subliminally promoting Borden dairy products, and illustrating just how much the event had changed. Gone were the days of anonymous toy soldiers and farm animals. Broadway was now a stage for iconic commercial trademarks.

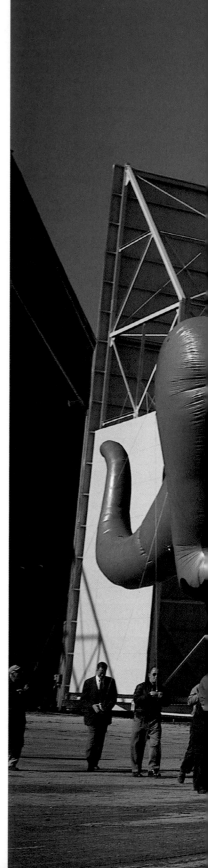

★ I've Never Even Met Fred Flintstone!

This is not Dino, denizen of Bedrock. This, like Elsie the Cow, is a trademark, the Sinclair Oil apatosaurus (known as a brontosaurus back in the 1960s). Also as with Elsie, the dinosaur was built to entertain and to direct folks to the upcoming World's Fair, where Sinclair would mount the extraordinary Dinoland exhibit. Nine huge fiberglass dinosaurs, three of them animated, sought to replicate life on earth 165 million years ago, while a 70-foot-long apatosaurus peered down from the roof of the Sinclair pavilion, beckoning fair-goers and scaring the daylights out of drivers on the adjacent Grand Central Parkway. The Macy's dino, benign by contrast, was taken for a leisurely test stroll at the Goodyear airfield in Akron.

Inset: New York Daily News

★ Don't Rain on Our Parade!

It certainly seems suitable in retrospect that the big new balloon in 1962 was Donald Duck: He was greeted by a day that only a duck might enjoy, as rain fell on the parade for most of the morning. The five principal presiders, baseball stars Willie Mays and Ralph Terry, golf great Arnold Palmer, football legend Otto Graham and former boxing champ Jack Dempsey, might have preferred a weather delay, but the show went on despite the downpour, keeping intact the parade's record of never yielding to wind or weather, only to war. Jimmy Durante, Carol Lawrence, Gene Krupa and Tony Bennett were troupers in entertaining the sodden spectators, as were these slickered band members, unbowed as they marched past Macy's. One year later, the parade would have its mettle tested by circumstances more dampening than rainfall.

★ In a World Recently Hardened by Reality, Fantasy Returns

Certainly there was discussion whether the parade should proceed. On November 22, 1963, the President of the United States, John F. Kennedy, had been killed while traveling through Dallas in a convertible limousine. The country was still in mourning, and Thanksgiving would fall only three days after the late President's internment in Arlington National Cemetery. What was the proper thing to do? Finally, Macy's president Dave Yunich said the parade would go on, so as not to disappoint "millions of children." Flags flew at half-staff, and black bunting was liberally applied to the floats. These two photos speak volumes, if subtly, about a day when only 1.4 million spectators, many fewer than normal, lined the route. Santa waves tiredly; his helpers appear downcast. A model of the Unisphere, symbol of a peaceful brotherhood of man, arrives at Macy's, announcing the 1964 World's Fair and, perhaps, better days.

The Parade Gets Legs

★★ *If I ever got a chance to get a group of American girls who would be taller and have longer legs and could do really complicated tap routines and eye-high kicks—they'd knock your socks off!* ★★

— **Russell Markert, founder of the Rockettes**

They started not as the Rockettes but the Rockets, and not in New York but in St. Louis. There, in 1925—mere months after the Macy's Parade was born—choreographer Russell Markert, who had been wowed by the John Tiller Girls' performance in the latest Ziegfeld Follies show, sought to assemble his own female precision dance team—but taller, with longer legs. He had a firm vision for his Missouri Rockets: wholesome "dancing daughters," emanating spirit and pizzazz, a group, certainly, but always seeming to be "one dancer." Illusion was a key. There was the illusion that all those limbs belonged to a single organism, another illusion that all those girls were the same height. (They weren't. The trick was to put the tallest dancers in the center, the shortest on the ends.)

The Missouri Rockets conquered St. Louis, then took their act on the road. Very much impressed was a quintessential New York City impresario named Samuel L. "Roxy" Rothafel. During the Roarin' '20s and early '30s, Roxy had his fingers in a number of Big Apple pies. His *Roxy and His Gang* variety show, broadcast from the Capitol Theatre, was popular on NBC radio, and his new Roxy Theater was a grand showbiz palace. It wasn't a far leap for Rothafel to rename Markert's squad the Roxyettes after he convinced them that a long and glorious future could be enjoyed in Manhattan. It was another easy jump to dub them the Rockettes when they helped open Rothafel and the Rockefeller family's glorious new venue, the Radio City Music Hall, on December 27, 1932.

Ray Bolger and the Flying Wallendas were among 17

To become a modern-day Rockette, like these seen at the parade's terminus, a woman must be at least 18 years old, proficient in ballet, tap and jazz, able to kick the clouds from the sky and willing to wear a smile from dawn to dusk.

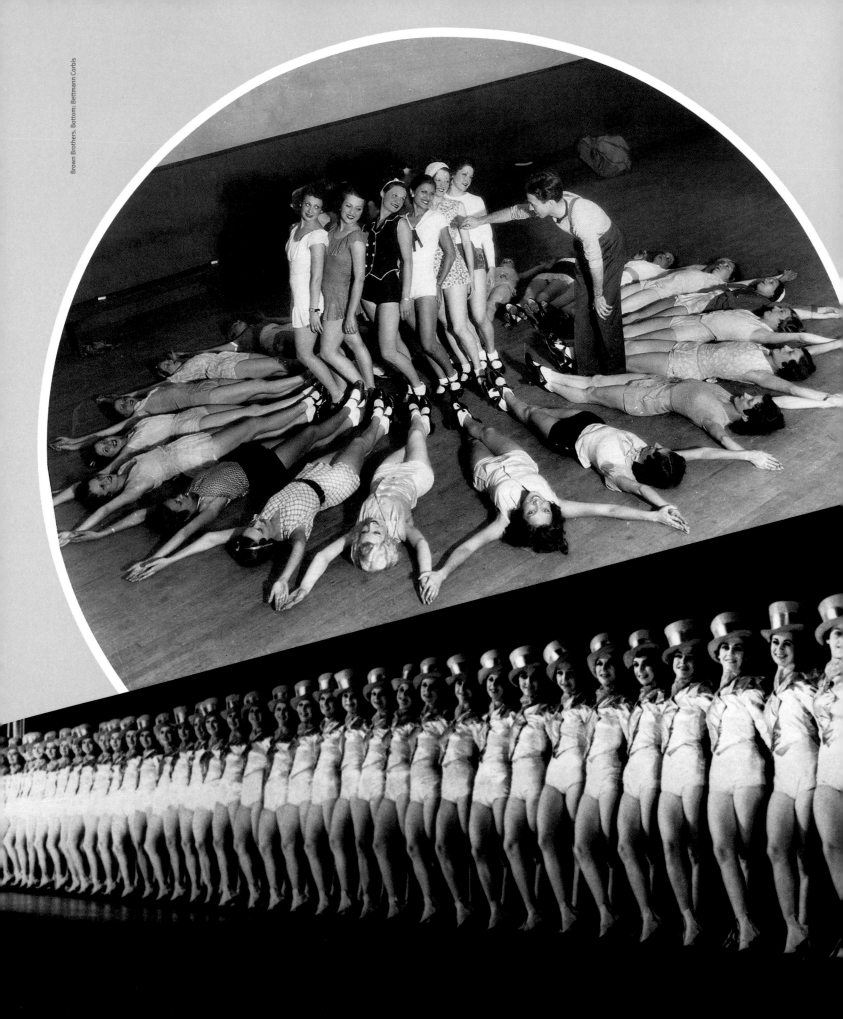

acts on the bill that night, but no one upstaged the 16 smiling, tapping Rockettes. They became, quite quickly, a New York fixture, and before very long they were an integral part of that venerable New York institution, the Radio City Christmas Spectacular. That show, with its Living Nativity tableau and the sensational "Parade of the Wooden Soldiers" number, choreographed by Markert, opened in 1933, beginning a tradition that, by millennium's end, would be enjoyed by 2.1 million people annually, in productions from midtown Manhattan to Chicago to Mexico City.

So as we see, these two iconic entertainment enterprises, the Macy's Thanksgiving Day Parade and the Radio City Rockettes, were finding their legs at almost exactly the same time. Yet they managed to avoid each other for more than three decades. When their paths finally did cross in 1958, it was clear at once that the match was made in heaven.

The Rockettes lent a *je ne sais quoi* to the parade that it didn't yet possess, and this assertion isn't meant leeringly. First, they brought a new and high form of artistry. The Rockettes were (and are) terrific dancers, and Markert's ideas of synchronized tap, many of which persevere in Rockette choreography today, demanded technical prowess and extraordinary athleticism. The great modern dancer Twyla Tharp became a big Rockettes fan upon landing in New York; she appreciated the excitement they generated and the fact that they were dancers who were having a great deal of fun. The preeminent American ballet critic Edwin Denby summed up the Rockette effect nicely in his definitive volume, *Looking at the Dance:* "Their cheerfulness

★ Markert's style, taught here by his principal assistant, Gene Snyder, called for synchronicity and smiles. The blend is reflected even today, not only in Rockette routines but in the Ice Capades, which he also choreographed.

is sweet as that of a church social. Their dancing is fresh and modest, their rhythm accurate and light and everyone can see that they accomplish what they set out to do to perfection. At the end of the routine when the line of them comes forward in a precision climax, the house takes all thirty-six of them collectively to its family heart."

This is just what Macy's desired, regarding the far-flung American family: to be taken to its heart. Now it had a signature act that, like its airy balloons, its fanciful floats and its all-American marching bands, couldn't be a better fit. "And the Rockettes added to the Macy's audience, too," said Jean McFaddin, the famous Parade Lady who served as director of the extravaganza from 1977 through the year 2000. "At least until the Rockettes performed

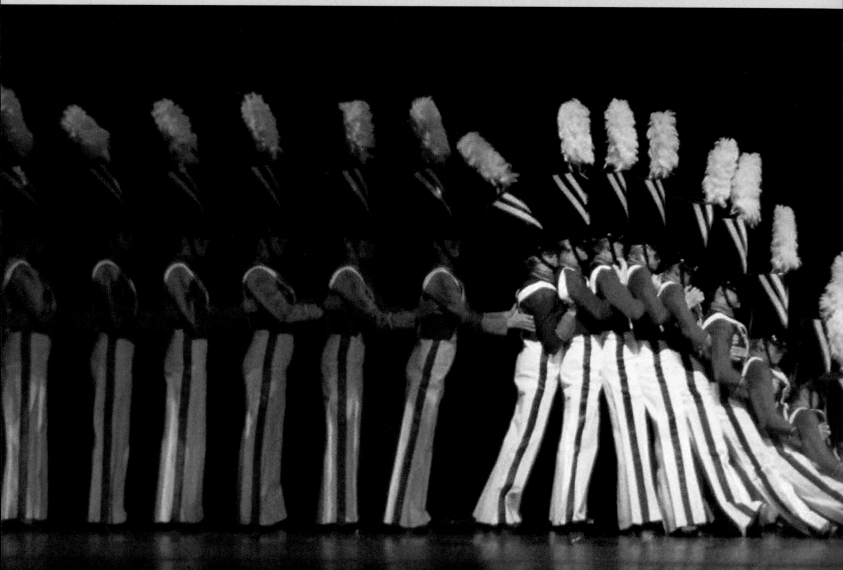

★ The 1958 Rockettes posed as Christmas stockings (opposite). They should have stuck with the look. Although their domino effect goes over big on the Music Hall stage, when the dancers wore pants to Macy's, the viewing audience voted thumbs down.

on television, half the fathers of America would sit alongside their little girls in front of the tube, waiting for that big moment."

This isn't about sex, precisely. As Denby correctly wrote, "the Rockettes avoid what is 'hot' and disturbing in taps." What this is about is the dream girl next door. It is also about little girls dreaming of growing up (to at least 5' 6 $\frac{1}{2}$", if not more than 5' 10 $\frac{1}{2}$", as stipulated in the Rockette rules), of traveling to the big city, of nailing the audition, of realizing the impossible aspiration of becoming … a Rockette. Since 1932 more than 2,000 American girls have made it to the stage of Radio City, a journey that is, in its terpsichorean way, as magical as Santa Claus's visit.

The last thing anyone would ever do then is tamper with the illusion. Mess with the dream.

Right?

"The only year we ever got complaints about the Rockettes was the year when they wanted to be different," recalled McFaddin. "All of America is sitting there, waiting for the zip, waiting for the glamour, and out come the Rockettes in these uniforms. No legs showing. The Rockettes without legs. And then their routine has this punchline where they all fall down, like dominoes. Well, I'll tell you, America was not overjoyed. The letters poured in, and it became very important to us that they go back to their traditional role the next Thanksgiving."

That role has included, through the years, serving as Santa's cortege and as his greeters at 34th Street. It no longer involves traveling the entire parade route, since the Rockettes' schedule at Radio City has grown to as many as six Christmas Spectaculars per day during the holiday season. "They show up on time, keep warm in the trailers, come out on cue, sometimes make their way through the snow in their tap shoes, do their kick, get back on the bus and head uptown," said McFaddin.

That sounds very businesslike, but what the Rockettes leave behind each year is a bit of fantasy and magic. They sprinkle their special fairy dust.

New York's parade went national, then international, and by 1968 a band whose regular gig was at Buckingham Palace moonlighted in the sunshine of Herald Square.

Marching On

1964–1976

It outlasted bell-bottoms. It outlasted the frug. It outlasted clogs, and, thank goodness, the parade outlasted disco.

It was sometimes tricky in the 1960s and '70s for the parade not to seem out of step. While a generation weaned on repeats of *Miracle on 34th Street* was now heading upstate to Woodstock for its entertainment, every Thanksgiving morning Macy's had wholesome Lorne Greene and Betty White presenting, and nary a concession to times that had been a-changin' for a while. But if the parade began to appear quaint or perhaps silly to growing Boomers, this hardly mattered. The Thanksgiving Day show wasn't really for them, not anymore. It was for the kids who had replaced them, and then the kids who would replace those. The parade wasn't concerned with Vietnam and civil strife, it was concerned with a fantasy America peopled with elves, clowns and gargantuan flying animals. In this way, it was true to itself, and smart for the long haul. The Boomers would be back someday, their own wee ones in tow.

Linus the Lionhearted enjoyed a strange animated career. The King of Beasts started as a pitchman for Post Crispy Critters. Voiced by Sheldon Leonard, and with sidekicks played by Carl Reiner and Jonathan Winters, Linus got a Saturday morning TV gig in 1964, the same year he was test-flown for his debut in the parade. Linus's last show aired in 1969 but his balloon was more durable, airing as recently as 1991.

In 1960, New Jersey native Manfred Bass, hoping for a career as a children's book illustrator, heard that Macy's was looking for a designer. "Next thing I knew," he recalled years later, "I was sculpting a dragon." Working out of Macy's Special Productions studio—a massive space within a former Tootsie Roll factory in Jersey's Hoboken— Bass, over 40 years, created several balloons and scores of gorgeous floats. He more than anyone was responsible for the bright and beautiful look of the modern parade. In 1969, Bass, in overalls, and fellow float-builder David Uhlig sent in the clown (opposite).

AUTUMN SPLENDOR FLOAT

35' LONG 21' WIDE 16' HIGH
TOTAL of 6 BUTTERFLIES GIR
DRAWN BY M. BASS 1965

Nedick's

Joel Elkins

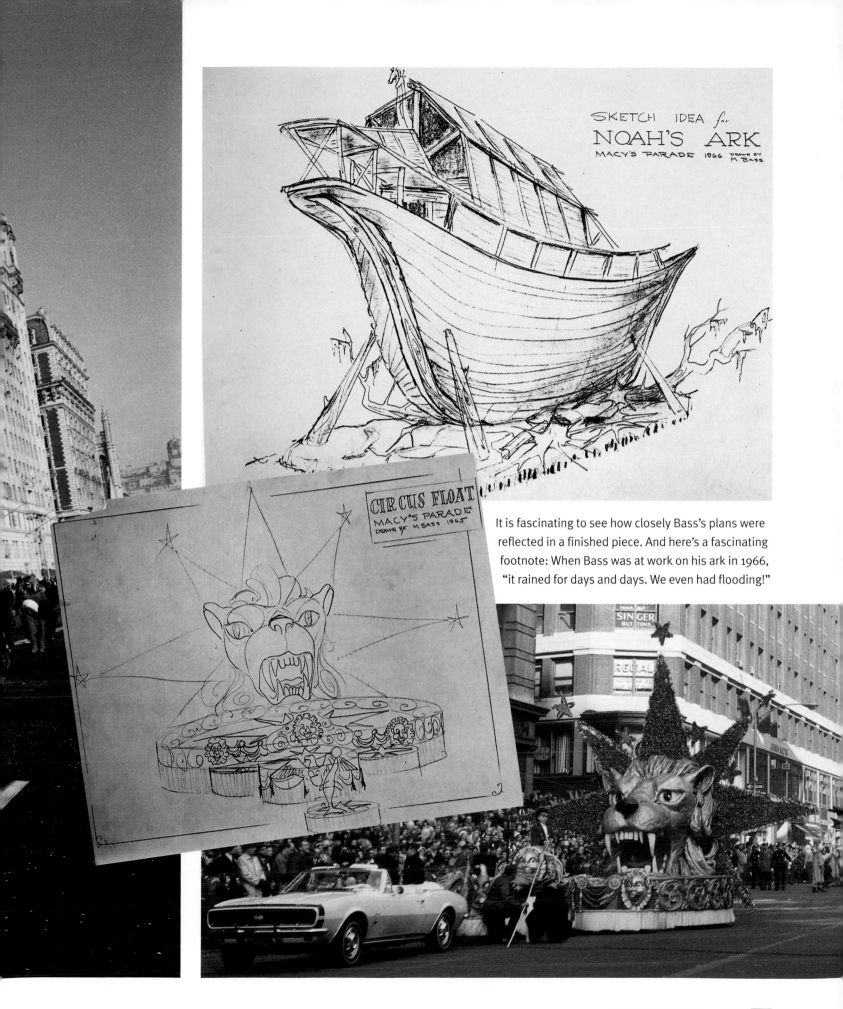

SKETCH IDEA for NOAH'S ARK
MACY'S PARADE 1966 DRAWN BY M BASS

CIRCUS FLOAT
MACY'S PARADE
DRAWN BY M. BASS 1965

It is fascinating to see how closely Bass's plans were reflected in a finished piece. And here's a fascinating footnote: When Bass was at work on his ark in 1966, "it rained for days and days. We even had flooding!"

UNDERDOG
TOTAL TELEVISION
PRODUCTIONS INC.
366 MADISON AVENUE
NEW YORK, NEW YORK

★ There's No Need to Fear!

As a cartoon character he may have been an Underdog, kind of a minor-league canine Superman, but as a balloon he was a big-league superstar. He joined the lineup in 1965 and became an immediate fan favorite; he remains, with Felix the Cat, Spider-Man, Bullwinkle and a few others, one of the inflatables most closely associated with the parade. At 64 feet long, he was a stable flier, and he certainly was colorful, but the source of the pooch's outsized popularity remains a mystery. Call it charisma. The old dog lasted in the parade until '84. Here, as a pup, he took a practice swing in Akron one month before his rookie season.

★ A Peaceful End to a Tumultuous Year

In 1968, Popeye was preceded in the line of march by a posse of cowgirls, and trailed only by the big guy. The *Daily News* caption on the photo above read: "As Popeye, who was followed by Santa Claus, helps bring parade to close, four youngsters are left with memories to dream on." The words seemed to reflect the fact that the parade, and Thanksgiving Day itself, were again providing balm for a country in despair. Martin Luther King Jr. and Bobby Kennedy had been assassinated, and the riots in Chicago at the Democratic convention were only the most famous of many violent clashes in the U.S. The Vietnam war was in full swing, recently elected Richard Nixon was headed for Washington, and no one knew what the future held for wistful children such as these.

★ **Can You Guess What Decade We're In?**

Right you are! There was much about the fashion sense of the 1970s that may appear, today, lamentable. But if you were a big, vibrant parade, there was everything right with splashy colors, psychedelic patterns and hap-hap-happy faces. The bumblebee car below and the odd, bigheaded creature at left, who seems to have popped from a Lewis Carroll nightmare, both took part in the 1970 parade. That ubiquitous symbol of the disco decade, the yellow smiley face, gazed down upon the parade-goers in 1972.

★ The Spirit of '76

These minutemen stood and delivered during the 1975 parade, aiming for the upcoming bicentennial. In New York City during the year of living patriotically, Macy's made quite as big a splash with its extraordinary fireworks display on the Fourth of July as it did with the parade. Then, in 1977, the Thanksgiving Day pageant got a renewal of focus—and a redirection. Hired that year to head the store's Special Productions Department was Jean McFaddin, a spirited Texan with a theatrical manner and a theatrical background. "I decided to not change anything my first year, just to watch the parade and look around," she reminisced in 2001, on the occasion of her retirement after 24 years as the Parade Lady. "Then, after the parade was over, I set my sights on Santa. I decided I had to deal with him first."

Globe Photos (2)

The Stars Come Out

★★ *When we'd invite celebrities, we found the parade was part of their childhood, too. They became kids again, and ran for their floats.* ★★

— Jean McFaddin, the Parade Lady

The leading lights of stage, screen and television lend a special glow to the Macy's parade. But the event was already 10 years old before the first nationally known personality made an appearance. In 1934 a balloon bearing the visage of singer-actor Eddie Cantor joined the fun. When the procession passed the marquee at 34th Street, "Banjo Eyes" himself, a true superstar of the day, was there smiling and waving. While Eddie's balloon was the first and last to carry the image of a living person, the parademeisters were delighted with the attention that Cantor aroused, and decided to bring in more stars in future parades.

The following year, Brillo-haired Harpo Marx, happy to promote the brothers' latest flick, *A Night at the Opera,* brought his madcap excitement to the festivities, and the famous big-band leader Paul Whiteman showed up as well. Two years later, Whiteman's colleague Benny Goodman made the swinging scene, and in 1941 Dinah Shore sang carols from the marquee. The only entertainment during the war years was provided by New York's effervescent mayor Fiorello La Guardia, who, in helping Macy's donate rubber from its balloons to the cause,

★ Eternal showstopper Ann Miller wowed 'em on Broadway in 1979. Much earlier, in 1951, William Boyd, a.k.a. Hopalong Cassidy, worked the street atop Topper.

★ **Three songbirds: Dusty Springfield sang "You Don't Have to Say You Love Me" in '66. Christina Aguilera waved to fans in '99. In 1979 Miss Ross, diva to the core, toured the Big Apple on a big apple. Opposite: From 1962 to '72, hosts Lorne Greene and Betty White were to Macy's what Bob Hope was to the Oscars.**

"slew" a green dragon with a knife.

The cast of *Miracle on 34th Street* brightened the affair in 1947, and life imitated art as Edmund Gwenn reprised his turn as the parade's Santa. Milton Berle, attired as George Washington, closed out the decade when he served as Grand Marshal. Uncle Miltie would revisit 33 years later, in different garb. "He was Cinderella," remembered Jean McFaddin, parade director during Berle's second turn. "We got so many letters from people upset that a man was in drag in the Macy's Parade. Hello! Milton Berle made his living in drag!"

Peter Pan was brought to Broadway as a musical in 1950 by Leonard Bernstein. Boris Karloff was Captain Hook, and that year the Sultan of Scare himself, clad in his sequined Hook outfit, manned the helm of a pirate ship float. For many, 1953 remains the quintessential Thanksgiving Day parade. A celestial array of stars had become a priority, and there was sparkle galore: Sid Caesar and Imogene Coca, Steve Allen, Martha Raye, Wally Cox and

Howdy Doody. Celeste Holm was a darling Little Bo Peep. Jack Frost paid a call the next year, and most everyone except the majorettes followed the advice of the parade's guiding fathers and wore woolen underwear. The lovely Virginia Mayo and Judy Holliday were among those who stayed toasty.

Danny Kaye was Grand Marshal in '55, dressed as a court jester on the Valentine float and accompanied by a queen on a plush red-and-white throne: his nine-year-old daughter, Dena. Sometimes, the celebrities in the parade aren't from the showbiz world, but are special for other reasons. Also in '55, 13-year-old Anthony Griffith, recently arrived from Sydney to get treatment for mus-

cular dystrophy, was given a special viewing stand for his wheelchair. Four years thereafter, a nine-year-old girl, described in the *Times* as "looking slightly seasick," was a special eminence indeed aboard her boat float. She was Emily Severance Grinnell of New Bedford, Massachusetts, and the great-great-granddaughter of one Emily Morgan. When R.H. Macy had gone to sea as a cabin boy more than a hundred years before the advent of Emily Grinnell, he had left Nantucket on a whaler named for Emily Morgan.

In 1959 Shirley Temple Black, escorted by her three children, wore a white mink and a glittery tiara on the Story Book float. It was a bone-chilling day, but her husband, Charles, marched beside her the whole way. "They really cranked up a parade here, didn't they?" he exulted. "The children are very excited. This is their first trip to New York."

Such enthusiasm was welcomed by parade officials, of course, but could cause trouble. "The prob-

Kelly/Mooney/Corbis

lem we had with some stars was trying to keep them from wanting to come back year after year—there wouldn't be room for all of them," said McFaddin. "They had such fun, they wanted to reserve their place." Bob Hope proved a merry King of the Parade in 1960, when he was ably assisted by the cast of the top-rated TV oater *Bonanza*. Much later, recalling how fine the experience had been, Hope was happy to return to the parade, and this time brought his wife. "He was old by then," remembered McFaddin. "So we had a special plastic casing for the float. Everyone thought it was bulletproof glass, like the Popemobile. They were won-

dering why Bob and Dolores needed protection. Actually, it was just to keep in the heat."

A tradition was begun in 1961 when sports legends Willie Mays, Jack Dempsey, Arnold Palmer and Otto Graham joined in the celebration. From that year on, athletes would always be included, typically batting champions, Super Bowl winners and hometown heroes like the Yankees and Mets.

There have been, in more recent years, magic acts—in both 1974 and '75, Doug Henning unsheathed his splendid style of prestidigitation—and many, many music acts. Only Diana Ross's aristocratic beauty prevented her from resembling a worm when she wore a bright green suit and sang atop a two-story-tall apple in '75. "Most singers just lip-synched their songs," said McFaddin. "Not Jessye Norman, the opera star. The rain was pouring, and it was cold. I was worried about her voice. But she insisted on singing, and let me tell you, she sang." McFaddin remembered other situations with her singers—the year the littlest Osmond could hold it no longer and required a change of trousers; the year a Roberta Flack impersonator showed up and tried to steal the star's spot on a float. But her favorite concerned Ricky Martin's old boy band, Menudo. "They were big, like the Beatles," she said. "They wanted to sing at the parade. We couldn't put them on a float, we would have had a riot. Only three people knew they were going to perform. I hid them in a loading dock, and then the bus drove into Herald Square and they played on top of the bus. Then we drove them out of there—fast.

"That was the biggest sensation I can recall. Except Santa, of course. That's why we did away with Grand Marshals. This is Santa's parade. Even Menudo can't top Santa."

★ Opposite page: Bob and Dolores stayed warm in their Hopemobile. In 1952, Grand Marshal Jackie Gleason posed with fellow TV stars Jock "Range Rider" Mahoney and Jack Sterling of the show *Big Top*.

★ Men of action:
Tap dancing Ben Vereen was resplendent in tails in 1975, the same year daredevil Evel Knievel popped a wheelie on Broadway. In 1969, Mets relievers Tug McGraw and Ron Taylor were still afloat after their truly amazin' World Series triumph.

The Eternal Parade

Mike Albans/New York Daily News

1977– FOREVER

Tested by tragedy in 1997 when the Cat in the Hat balloon crashed, causing injury, the parade paused, reflected, tweaked itself and headed for a limitless future.

The pageant is, now, indispensable. It is as inconceivable to have a Thanksgiving without the Macy's parade as it would be to have a Fourth of July without fireworks, a New Year's Eve without champagne or a Christmas without Santa. By its 75th marching in 2001, the parade had survived wind, weather, war, societal and cultural shifts, and even an episode of frightening mishap. But no circumstance could dislodge it from the heart and mind of the American family. This, finally, was perhaps the source of its power: It was a family affair. It enchanted young ones on the Manhattan curbside and on the floor in front of the TV set in Kansas even as, in its ripe old age, it began to have a curious effect on parents and grandparents. These oldsters would smile, happy for the children—and also pleased to remember what life was like when they saw their own first Macy's Day Parade.

On November 6, 1999, the Honey Nut Bee was hangin' in Hoboken, New Jersey, with those good dogs Snoopy and Blue. All passed their tests and flew in the parade weeks later.

★ The Torch Passes

Marionette artist Tony Sarg was Bil Baird's mentor at
Macy's. Years later, Baird's puppetry on television was
inspirational to a boy growing up in Mississippi named
Jim Henson: *That's what I want to do.* In 1955, Henson,
only 19, created a character that he considered his alter
ego, a frog named Kermit. Twenty-two years on, Kermit,
by then the most famous of Henson's marvelous
Muppets, was tapped for the Macy's parade by Jean
McFaddin as her first choice for a new balloon. Designers
and other craftsmen in the Engineered Fabrics division of
Goodyear Aerospace in Rockmart, Georgia, went to work.

Throughout 1977 and into '78, Kermit took shape. At times it appeared Goodyear was building a tribute to *Jaws*, or to that man-eating plant in *Little Shop of Horrors*. A scale-model Kermit moved about the plant to keep everyone's eyes on the prize.

In 1978 the helium-filled Kermit was test-flown in Rockmart and was paid a visit by the hand-filled Kermit, who was taping a spot for his hit television series, *The Muppet Show*. In the fall the big green balloon made its first appearance in New York City, and then in the following spring it became the parade's first ambassador to England when it entertained the kiddies at the Queen's Children's Party in London.

Christopher Morris/Black Star

★ Able to Leap Tall Buildings at a Single Bound (Or Slide Serenely Between Them)

Superman, a perennial favorite, has had more than one incarnation in the parade; in fact, he made his Macy's debut before World War II. Of the various versions, the 1980 model (left) was the most supercolossal at 100 feet in length, one of the largest balloons ever. This Superman was a fitting swan song for Goodyear's half-century association with the parade. (The tiremaker went out of the balloon business in 1981.) Above: The Man of Steel—well, the Man of Rubber—cruised Manhattan in 1984.

★ Chillin' on the Upper West Side

The parade that once commenced uptown in Harlem now begins at 77th Street. On Thanksgiving eve, a mile-long caravan of trucks makes its way from Macy's Hoboken warehouse through the Lincoln Tunnel to New York City. Boxes weighing between 450 and 800 pounds are unloaded and opened. The synthetic creatures are laid on tarps that cover streets near the American Museum of Natural History. At three p.m. the public can enter the area to watch the stars of the show being fueled from tankers holding 120,000 cubic feet of gas. It's a surreal scene as the many separate chambers inflate (a recent Rugrats balloon, for instance, had 22 gas chambers requiring 16,780 cubic feet of gas; Yogi was a simpler organism). The show ends at about 10, and everyone beds down, with netting for blankets. Rise and shine is 5:30 a.m., when each balloon gets topped off.

★ Elements of the Modern Parade

The night before the parade has become ritualistic, as has the following dawn. For years now, every Thanksgiving morn has seen huge balloons such as Yogi and Mickey and the Pink Panther awakened from their slumbers and released from their nets. Even as they get their helium breakfast, bands muster and clowns limber up. Finally someone shouts: "Let's have a parade!" The Turkey float leads the way down Central Park West. Santa always trails. The balloons are handled by teams whose dress reflects the characters' colors. Once they reach 34th Street and 7th Avenue, the balloons are brought to street level, and like Mickey, they sag. Clowns and bands, too, are deflated.

★ Elements of the Modern Parade III

Because of the regulations put into place after the Cat in the Hat incident of 1997, balloons no longer fly as high as the Pink Panther did in '91, but they travel the same route adjacent to Central Park. As they do so, workers who have been up all night assembling the parade scurry downtown to 34th Street, where they begin to dismantle everything that comes their way. This includes hundreds and hundreds of "float elements," which, when spread out the previous night, covered more than 70,000 square feet on nine city blocks. Far too busy to watch the parade, the workers will gather on Friday in the Hoboken warehouse with other parade staffers and their families to view the previous day's proceedings on video and at last savor a Thanksgiving feast.

☞ **Open here**

Joe McNally

★ **Learning the Sophisticated Art of Clowning**

Despite the glowing smiles on the faces of Garfield's friends, a clown's lot is not always a happy one. The 500 greasepainted volunteers have to awaken before dawn and get to the 77th Street start line by 7:30 a.m. If Thanksgiving comes up cold, the clowns have to do some serious jumping and hopping to stay warm. Long trained in these and other, sillier movements, they have for decades attended "clown school." Dick Monday, a former director of the Ringling Bros. and Barnum & Bailey Clown College, led a tutorial (opposite, top) in 1998.

Below, three masters: Adam Auslander and Hilary Chaplain of the Big Apple Circus Clown Care Unit, flanked Monday at the '98 sessions. A Monday rule of thumb: "Clowns can't play down to children. Kids are the most honest audience. If something isn't funny, they won't laugh."

WEST PARK MARKET

Spider-Man, seen here in 1991, was a star of the parade. His 78-foot figure was kept aloft by 8,300 cubic feet of helium in 10 chambers running down his back; his stomach chambers were filled with air. The Webbed One was retired after the 1998 parade.

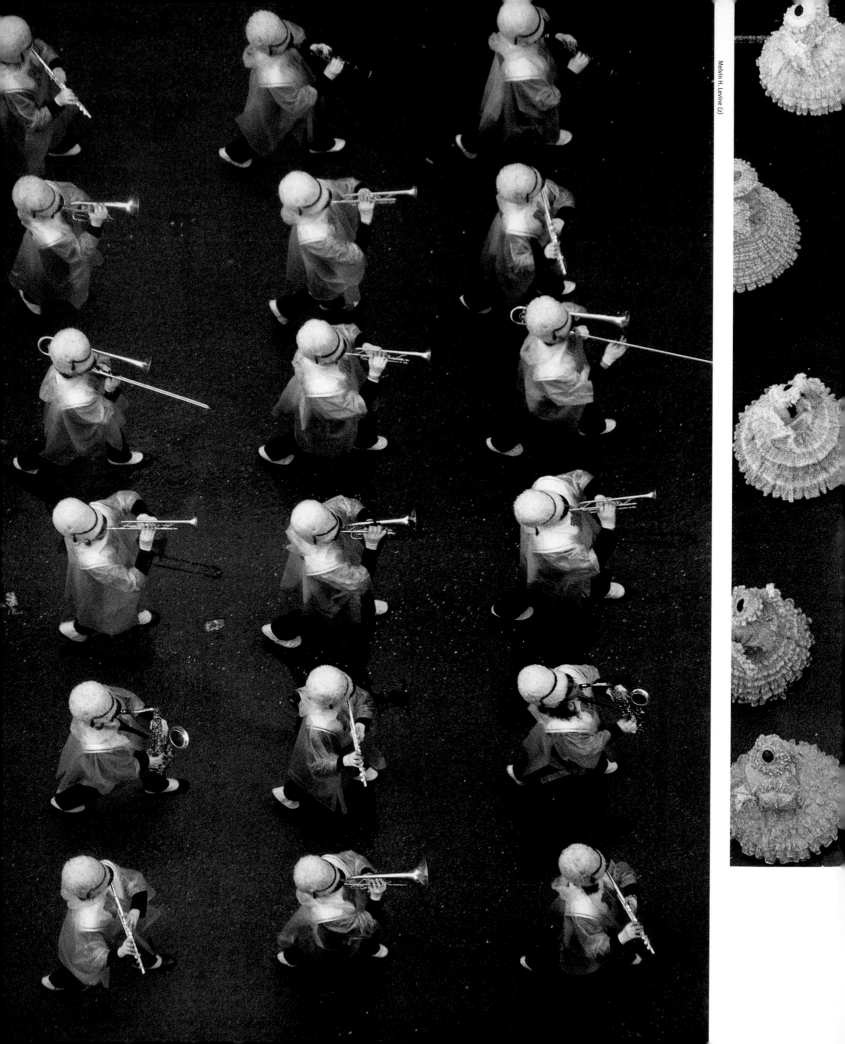

⭐ And the Band Played On

A morning rain in 1992 couldn't dampen the enthusiasm of 15 marching bands and their colleague cheerleaders, majorettes and dancers. As seen from on high, the slickers and slick streets actually added a lovely sheen to many of the parade's patterns. This '92 edition was dedicated to the thousands of Macy's volunteers who worked it that year—some of them traveling from stores as far-flung as Washington, D.C., and Burlington, Vermont—and to the many thousands more who had volunteered since the first employees' parade in 1924.

★ A Big, Big Dog and One Bad, Bad Boy

Storybook characters in the pageant used to list toward Mother Goose. These days they are, for the most part, contemporary heroes like Clifford the Big Red Dog. Indeed, they are often dogs, traveling in a sizable pack—Clifford, Snoopy, Blue. "One year we had eight pooches," said Jean McFaddin. "Thank God for Garfield!" (That was then, this is now: The very fat cat is out of the lineup, having headed for the balloon retirement home after the 1999 parade.) Clifford, as any child could tell you, was a star of page and screen, while that skateboarding dude Bart Simpson was a boob-tuber of the first water. He was also one of the parade's Gen-X classics.

★ Old Friends and New Friends

As the parade headed toward, then into, the new millennium, animated venerables like Woody Woodpecker and Bugs Bunny finally made their appearances (Woody flew from 1982 until 1997; Bugs from 1989 to 1992). Several up-to-date stars were also recruited. Izzy the torchbearing mascot (below, left) heralded the 1996 Atlanta Olympics. Garfield the cat lasted from 1984 through 1999. Opposite: Blue's Clues' Blue took his cue in 1999. Movie star Babe the pig debuted in 1998. And Arthur the aardvark, star of Marc Brown's books and his own eponymous PBS series, first said hello to the kids below in 1997.

Sara Krulwich/The New York Times

Gail Mooney/Corbis

★ In the End, It's About the Kids—and Santa

Every year, there's a tot or two who need direction. Since 1924, they've all been hoping for a glimpse of the parade's ultimate star, Santa Claus. According to Macy's, the man in the sleigh, from that very first year, has been "Kris Kringle"—none other than and no other than. This will not be disputed. However, it should be noted that there have been rumors. One, for instance, is that in 1947, Kringle was unavoidably detained at the Pole—bad weather, it seems—and that his place in the parade was taken by Edmund Gwenn, the actor who won an Oscar for impersonating Kris in *Miracle on 34th Street*. Other gossip has it that, whenever Santa has had conflicts in recent years—years dating back to the 1960s—his fill-in has been a white-bearded, now semi-retired, still very jolly Macy's employee.

Another View

★ **Elliott Erwitt's Parade**

Encouraged by winning a young-photographer's contest in 1951, Elliott Erwitt began taking pictures in earnest—fascinating, often funny pictures, which found their way into LIFE and other magazines. Having moved to Manhattan's West Side in 1965, he took up a Thanksgiving tradition shared by his neighbors: "Everybody has parade parties. We invite our needy friends from the Upper East Side." One year Erwitt caught the Pink Panther sneaking up on the young boys across the way. Another time, two of his daughters, Sasha and Amy, were unsuspecting as Snoopy gave them the eye (following page). "There was no planning or anything," Erwitt recalled. "You have a camera, you take a picture. You see what comes out." The perspective seen here is no longer. "We live on the eighth floor," he said. "The balloons aren't allowed to fly this high anymore. Some things change. Our party's mostly grandchildren now. And we look down at the balloons."

Elliott Erwitt/Magnum